TORONTO MEDIEVAL LATIN TEXTS 33

TORONTO MEDIEVAL LATIN TEXTS

SAMUEL PRESBITER

Notes from the School of William de Montibus

Collecta ex diuersis auditis in scola magistri Willelmi de Monte

Edited from

Oxford, Bodleian Library

MS Bodley 860

by

ANDREW N.J. DUNNING

Published for the

CENTRE FOR MEDIEVAL STUDIES

by the

PONTIFICAL INSTITUTE OF MEDIAEVAL STUDIES

Toronto

Library and Archives Canada Cataloguing in Publication

Samuel, Presbiter, flourished 1200, author
Notes from the school of William de Montibus = Collecta ex diuersis auditis in scola magistri Willelmi de Monte / Samuel Presbiter ; edited from Oxford, Bodleian Library MS Bodley 860 by Andrew N.J. Dunning.

(Toronto medieval Latin texts ; 33)
Includes bibliographical references and index.
Issued in print and electronic formats.
Text in Latin; introduction and notes in English.
ISBN 978-0-88844-483-7 (paperback). – ISBN 978-1-77110-375-6 (pdf)

1. Samuel, Presbiter, flourished 1200. 2. William, de Montibus, approximately 1140–1213. 3. Pastoral theology – Early works to 1800. 4. Pastoral theology – History of doctrines – Middle Ages, 600–1500. 5. Poetry in Christian education – History – Medieval, 500–1500. 6. Christian poetry, Latin (Medieval and modern). 7. Learning and scholarship – History – Medieval, 500–1500. 8. Education, Medieval. 9. Bodleian Library. Manuscript. Bodley 860. I. Dunning, Andrew N. J., editor II. Pontifical Institute of Mediaeval Studies, issuing body III. Bodleian Library. Manuscript. Bodley 860 IV. Title. V. Title: Collecta ex diuersis auditis in scola magistri Willelmi de Monte. VI. Series: Toronto medieval Latin texts ; 33

BV4009.S24 2016 253 C2016-900431-7
C2016-900432-5

The Pontifical Institute of Mediaeval Studies
59 Queen's Park Crescent East
Toronto, Ontario, Canada M5S 2C4
www.pims.ca

MANUFACTURED IN CANADA

PREFACE

The TORONTO MEDIEVAL LATIN TEXTS series is published for the Centre for Medieval Studies, University of Toronto, by the Pontifical Institute of Mediaeval Studies. The series offers affordable editions suitable for university-level courses in medieval Latin. In approving projects, the editorial board bears in mind the pedagogical utility of the texts proposed.

At the same time, the series also aims to further original research by publishing previously unedited texts extant in single manuscripts, as well as more widely attested texts here edited from single manuscripts carefully chosen for their particular textual, historical, and codicological interest and importance, in recognition that the scribal makers of such versions were important participants in the ongoing development of the text. Throughout the series, the base manuscript is emended only to restore sense, not to reconstruct an original authorial version; the minimal textual apparatus omits variants irrelevant to the integrity of the selected manuscript. Manuscript orthography and syntax are carefully preserved.

The Editorial Board, beyond merely supervising, takes responsibility for reviewing all proposals, for examining all specimens of volume editors' work, and for final reading of all editions published. It decides on all matters of editorial policy.

As General Editor, I would like to express my gratitude to the Centre for Medieval Studies for sponsorship of the series; to the Press of the Pontifical Institute and its unfailingly cordial and astute staff, particularly Fred Unwalla; to A.G. Rigg, whose sustained and tireless work as General Editor of the series for its first thirty volumes set a daunting standard to emulate; to Anna Burko, whose care and precision as Editorial Assistant did so much to maintain the standards of the series for over thirty years; to Philippa Matheson, whose expert work as Editorial Assistant continues so reassuringly to support the series. Finally, I am deeply indebted to all members of the editorial board, past and present, for the generosity of their sustained involvement, without which the series could not exist.

D.T.

ACKNOWLEDGEMENTS

This project began at a suggestion from Joseph Goering, whose tactful advice always turns out to be even more insightful than one first realizes. He generously read the text at several stages of its development and made many astute suggestions; Michael Gervers also encouraged the work at an early stage. The TMLT editorial board improved the book immensely, especially its reviewers, Alexander Andrée and Greti Dinkova-Bruun. A grant from the Social Sciences and Humanities Research Council of Canada allowed me to examine the manuscript in Oxford. While I was there, James Carley and Ann Hutchison most generously opened their flat as a base for studies; James Willoughby and Richard Sharpe produced many excellent leads. Thanks are also due to the Keeper of Special Collections for permission to study and photograph the manuscript at the Bodleian Library. My deepest gratitude is owed to Susan, who gladly spent many hours discussing medieval history and points of Latin grammar.

A.N.J.D.

ABBREVIATIONS

CCCM	Corpus Christianorum, continuatio Mediaevalis (Turnhout 1966–).
CCSL	Corpus Christianorum, series Latina (Turnhout 1953–).
CSEL	Corpus scriptorum ecclesiasticorum Latinorum (Vienna 1866–).
DMLBS	R.E. Latham, D.R. Howlett, and R.K. Ashdowne, eds. *Dictionary of Medieval Latin from British Sources* (Oxford 1975–2013).
Glosa	*Biblia latina cum glossa ordinaria: Facsimile reprint of the editio princeps, Adolph Rusch of Strassburg 1480/81*. Ed. Margaret T. Gibson and Karlfried Froehlich. 4 vols (Turnhout 1992). *Glosa interl.* refers to the interlinear gloss; *Glosa marg.* to the marginal.
PL	Patrologiae cursus completus, series Latina. 222 vols (Paris 1841–1865).
Rolls Series	Rerum Britannicarum medii aevi scriptores. 253 vols (London 1858–1911).
SC	R.W. Hunt, Falconer Madan, and P.D. Record. *A Summary Catalogue of Western Manuscripts in the Bodleian Library at Oxford*. 7 vols in 8 (Oxford 1895–1953).
Vulg.	*Biblia Sacra iuxta Vulgatam versionem*. Ed. Robert Weber et al. 5th ed. (Stuttgart 2007).

MAJOR WORKS OF SAMUEL PRESBITER

Ad habendam memoriam	*Collecta ad habendam memoriam quorumdam utilium in sacra scriptura*
Ex auditis super psalmos	*Collecta ex auditis super psalmos in scola magistri Willelmi de Monte*
Ex diuersis auditis	*Collecta ex diuersis auditis in scola magistri Willelmi de Monte*
Ex speculo cum uersibus	*Collecta ex speculo beati Gregorii cum uersibus*
Ex speculo sine uersibus	*Collecta ex speculo beati Gregorii sine uersibus*

OTHER ABBREVIATIONS

add.	addition/added
corr.	corrector/correction/corrected
eras.	erased/erasure
fol./fols	folio/folios
marg.	margin
MS	manuscript
om.	omitted
subst.	substituted

EDITORIAL SIGNS

⟨...⟩	signal letters supplied by the editor
***	indicate unreadable letters

CONTENTS

INTRODUCTION

'Hec sunt collecta ex diuersis auditis in scola magistri Willelmi de Monte'—'These are collected from various things heard in the school of Master William de Montibus.'[1] This heading explains much about the collection (called *Ex diuersis auditis* hereafter), uniquely preserved in Oxford, Bodleian Library, MS Bodley 860. Its compiler, Samuel Presbiter, remains obscure, and it is difficult to distinguish the specific contributions of William and Samuel. It consists of a series of lessons on the practical significance of theology, interspersed with a series of playful verses to aid memorization.

Samuel Presbiter's *Collecta*

All that is certainly known of Samuel Presbiter is his claimed tutelage under William de Montibus, who taught at the cathedral school in Lincoln from the 1180s until some point before his death in 1213. A reference to the 'lingua Britanie' suggests that Samuel studied at William's school in Lincoln rather than at Paris.[2] Along with *Ex diuersis auditis*, Samuel records William's lectures on the Psalms in *Ex auditis super psalmos*. He asserts that he wrote *Ad habendam memoriam*, forming the last part of Bodley 860, after he left the school: 'Hec composita sunt post dicessum a scola' (fol. 108r). The only definite references to his name are the identical closing lines of the two manuscripts preserving his works: 'Expliciunt collecta Samuelis presbiteri,' as found in Bodley 860, fol. 206v and Cambridge, Pembroke College, MS 115, fol. 77r.[3] The line is

1 Oxford, Bodleian Library, MS Bodley 860, fol. 94r. Joseph Goering, *William de Montibus (c. 1140–1213): The Schools and the Literature of Pastoral Care*, Studies and Texts 108 (Toronto 1992), 5–7, notes that William was called both 'de Montibus' and 'de Monte.' The manuscript's abbreviation is slightly ambiguous, but suggests the latter form.

2 *Ex auditis super psalmos*, Bodley 860, fol. 59rb; Goering, *William de Montibus*, 499 n. 9.

3 Although some reference works refer to 'Samuel Presbyter,' this spelling was only introduced through a seventeenth-century addition to Pembroke College 115, fol. 1r; 'Samuel Presbiter' is the only recorded medieval spelling.

contemporary with the rest of the text in both cases, and in the Pembroke College manuscript it was first roughed in by a hand that might be Samuel's. They once belonged to the Benedictine abbey of Bury St Edmunds, and may also have been produced there in the first half of the thirteenth century.[4]

A few references in documentary sources might be uncertainly identified with the author, notably a 'Samuel de Ounebi' (Owmby by Spital, in Lincolnshire) who witnesses a charter alongside William de Montibus between 1196 and 1203;[5] this was presumably the resident of the 'mansionem Samuelis' found in Owmby by Spital around 1200–1210,[6] though one also finds a Samuel de Cartis (also recorded as Scartres and Chartres) there in 1230–1240.[7] The name 'Presbiter,' which is unusual but attached to others in the city of Lincoln, was sometimes used to translate the name 'Cohen,' leading Goering to suggest that Samuel may have been a Jewish convert, or from a family of converts;[8] Foster makes the same assumption of a 'Samuel Presbiter' living in Huntingdon.[9] Given that both of the manuscripts containing Samuel's works are from Bury St Edmunds, the author might somehow have been associated with the abbey. Like William de Montibus, Samson, abbot from 1182 until 1211, had studied in Paris and by the time of his death had attracted an unusually high number of masters to the abbey.[10] There was a

4 The manuscripts are briefly described in Rodney M. Thomson, 'The Library and Archives of Bury St. Edmunds Abbey' (PhD thesis, University of Sydney, 1974), 2:144 (Pembroke College 115) and 2:288–289 (Bodley 860).

5 C.W. Foster and Kathleen Major, eds, *The Registrum Antiquissimum of the Cathedral Church of Lincoln*, Publications of the Lincoln Record Society 27–29, 32, 34, 41, 42, 46, 51, 62, 67, 68 (Hereford 1931–1973), 4:32–33 (nos 1140/41).

6 Ibid., 4:31 (no. 1138).

7 Ibid., 4:33–35 (nos 1142/43).

8 Goering, *William de Montibus*, 45 n. 68.

9 Foster and Major, *The Registrum Antiquissimum of the Cathedral Church of Lincoln*, 3:200; Pipe Roll Society, ed., *Feet of Fines of the Tenth Year of the Reign of King Richard I, AD 1198 to AD 1199*, Publications of the Pipe Roll Society 24 (London 1900), 71 (no. 104) records him there in 1198.

10 Antonia Gransden, *A History of the Abbey of Bury St Edmunds, 1182–1256: Samson of Tottington to Edmund of Walpole*, Studies in the History of Medieval Religion 31 (Woodbridge, Suffolk 2007), 135–136.

magister Samuel at the nearby Benedictine abbey of St Benet at Holme in 1203,[11] whose abbot at the time, Ralph, acted as a papal judge delegate alongside Samson, as did Hugh of Lincoln.[12]

Samuel labels almost all his works 'collecta,' most combining verses with a prose commentary. Two works are in prose, which are probably his earliest:

- *Collecta ex auditis super psalmos in scola magistri Willelmi de Monte* (Bodley 860, fols 9r–93v), an incomplete commentary on the Psalms;[13]
- *Collecta ex speculo beati Gregorii sine uersibus* (Pembroke College 115, fols 47r–77r).

In most of his works, both verses and prose were copied together, the prose often an extract from another work to show precisely what Samuel is versifying, and written directly above the verses to which it applies. These include:

- the present work, *Collecta ex diuersis auditis in scola magistri Willelmi de Monte* (Bodley 860, fols 94r–107v);
- *Collecta ex speculo beati Gregorii cum uersibus* (Pembroke College 115, fols 1r–41v);
- *De oratione dominica* (Pembroke College 115, fols 41v–44v), a versification of Hugh of St Victor's *De quinque septenis*, from which Samuel copies the prose passages without citation;
- four short compositions (Pembroke College 115, fols 45r–46r), with the incipits:
  1. 'Est proprium domini mentem bene pacificare' (*8 lines*)
  2. 'Est uagus hic cuius animus non recta cupiscit' (*2 lines*)
  3. 'Flos bonus est actus hoc est spes fulgor odorque' (*12 lines*)
  4. 'Multiplex hominis patientia dicitur esse,' entitled 'De patientia' (*2 lines*).

11 J.R. West, ed., *St. Benet of Holme, 1020–1210*, Norfolk Record Society 2–3 (Fakenham, Norfolk 1932), 1:59 (no. 99).

12 Gransden, *History of the Abbey of Bury St Edmunds*, 77, 69.

13 Goering, *William de Montibus*, 501–503, prints the text of fol. 9r.

In two works, the verses stand on their own, with glosses added in the margins:

- *Collecta ad habendam memoriam quorumdam utilium in sacra scriptura* (Bodley 860, fols 108r–206v);[14]
- a verse paraphrase of Psalm 1 (Bodley 860, fols 1r–8v).[15]

The two *Ex speculo* works abridge the *Speculum beati Gregorii*, Adalbert of Metz's epitome of Gregory the Great's *Moralia in Iob*;[16] many copies of it existed in England, including one at Bury St Edmunds by the late twelfth century.[17] Samuel also refers to it in his paraphrase of Psalm 1 (for example, Bodley 860, fols 4r, 5r) and *Ad habendam memoriam* (fols 128v, 130r), which are probably among his latest works. While his verses centred around prose usually summarize either William de Montibus or another book, the marginal glosses reflect increased confidence to work directly with biblical texts as well as secondary theological works, and often amalgamate references to many titles rather than summarize a single source.

Modern readers are often troubled in understanding the authorship of books whose contents are largely derivative.[18] It is tempting to dismiss Samuel as a mere 'excerpter,'[19] or as

14 Listed alongside other works of this genre in Greti Dinkova-Bruun, 'Biblical Versifications from Late Antiquity to the Middle of the Thirteenth Century: History or Allegory?,' in *Poetry and Exegesis in Premodern Latin Christianity: The Encounter Between Classical and Christian Strategies of Interpretation*, ed. Willemien Otten and Karla Pollmann, Supplements to *Vigiliae Christianae* 87 (Leiden 2007) 333, 339–340.

15 Edited in part by Greti Dinkova-Bruun, 'Samuel Presbyter and the Glosses to His Versification of Psalm 1: An Anti-Church Invective?,' in *Florilegium mediaevale: Études offertes à Jacqueline Hamesse à l'occasion de son éméritat*, ed. José Francisco Meirinhos and Olga Weijers, Textes et études du moyen âge 50 (Louvain-la-Neuve 2009), 155–174.

16 Unedited, but studied in Lorenzo Valgimogli, *Lo* Speculum Gregorii *di Adalberto di Metz*, Archivum Gregorianum 8 (Florence 2006).

17 Richard Sharpe et al., eds, *English Benedictine Libraries: The Shorter Catalogues*, Corpus of British Medieval Library Catalogues 4 (London 1996), B13.48a.

18 For the classic case of Peter Lombard's *Sentences* and the commentaries written on it, see Philipp W. Rosemann, *The Story of a Great Medieval Book: Peter Lombard's* Sentences (Peterborough, ON 2007).

19 Josiah Cox Russell, *Dictionary of Writers of Thirteenth-Century England*, Bulletin of the Institute of Historical Research, Special Supplement 3

Brian Twyne thought, little more than a devotee of William de Montibus.[20] Samuel expresses his approach through couplets that frame both of his manuscripts. He presents each of these as *distinctiones*, allowing them to be read in four different ways. One at the beginning of Bodley 860 and Pembroke College 115 lauds the maintenance of the mind, that it may be put to good use;[21] they close with a bidding for the author and reader to pray for one another.[22] These volumes appear to have been purposefully designed as Samuel's collected works. *Ex auditis super psalmos* was originally a separate maunscript, and another couplet affirming Samuel's diligence in understanding what he has collected, and his trust in its worthiness, appears on what was originally its opening page (now fol. 9r).[23] These sentiments are typical of the medieval approach to writing and learning.[24]

Ex diuersis auditis and Its Authorship

Samuel structures *Ex diuersis auditis* under a series of headings, attaching to each of these a poem of one to eleven lines, with a commentary to explain its contents. It might seem odd to write a commentary on one's own writing, but this is not unique: Alexander Neckam's *Sacerdos ad altare*, for instance, is a collection of obtuse passages describing aspects of

---

(London 1936), 147 (s.v. 'Samuel Presbyter').

20 'Qui Gulielmi de Monte celeberrimi suo tempore Oxoniae theol. professoris auditor diligens et admirator extitit.' Quoted in Thomas Tanner, *Bibliotheca Britannico-Hibernica, siue, De scriptoribus, qui in Anglia, Scotia, et Hibernia ad saeculi XVII initium floruerunt, commentarius*, ed. David Wilkins (London 1748), 651.

21 Mens conseru { etur } per opus ne stulta uag } etur.
Sic studiis d { etur } ut que prosint oper } etur.
(Bodley 860, fol. 1r; Pembroke 115, fol. 1r.)

22 Hec qui coll { egit } eterna pace qui } escat.
Hec quicumque l { egit } oret simul ut requi } escat.
(Bodley 860, fol. 206v; Pembroke College 115, fol. 76r.)

23 Hec qui col { legi } studiose pleraque } legi.
Quedam que { legi } credite digna } legi.
(Bodley 860, fol. 9r.)

24 Cf. Mary J. Carruthers, *The Book of Memory: A Study of Memory in Medieval Culture*, Cambridge Studies in Medieval Literature 10, 2nd ed. (Cambridge 2008), 244–246.

everyday life, with a commentary to explain their unusual vocabulary and grammatical constructions.[25] Samuel's poems direct memorization to learn the subject at hand: 'memorato' (17.1, 44.3, 50.3), 'commemorato' (19.3), 'memora' (30.2, 33.5, 36.3), 'poteris reminisci' (51.4). This was a common device in didactic literature of this period, used for teaching everything from the Bible to grammar.[26] It was also a favourite tool of William de Montibus, and several of the poems in *Ex diuersis auditis* also appear in his similar work *Versarius*, where they have a much sparser commentary. As Samuel's other works written in this format tend to follow their sources closely, the work's opening heading should be read as documentation rather than a boast, indicating that it is an edited form of his teacher's instruction.

William de Montibus was born in Lincoln and studied theology in Paris. There, Peter Comestor was among his teachers, and he knew both Alexander Neckam and Gerald of Wales. In the 1180s, Hugh, the bishop of Lincoln, invited him to teach at the cathedral school, where he was chancellor from at least 1194 until his death in April 1213 in Scotland, while England was under interdict. He was the best-known intellectual of Lincoln until the rise of Robert Grosseteste, and the praise heaped upon him after his death portrays him as a beloved teacher.[27] The sixteenth-century antiquarian John Leland wrote, 'The age in which he lived was sorely plagued by the thorny subtleties of the sophists, but he surmounted these difficulties so well that he gained for himself, if not truly flowing eloquence, then at least the stylistic vigour and substance of things, which he studiously passed straight on to others.'[28] Keeping in mind Leland's ten-

25 Alexander Neckam, *Sacerdos ad altare*, ed. Christopher J. McDonough, CCCM 227 (Turnhout 2010).

26 Greti Dinkova-Bruun, 'The Verse Bible as Aide-Mémoire,' in *The Making of Memory in the Middle Ages*, ed. Lucie Doležalová, Later Medieval Europe 4 (Leiden 2010), 115–131; Vivien Law, 'Why Write a Verse Grammar?,' *Journal of Medieval Latin* 9 (1999) 46–76.

27 Goering, *William de Montibus*, 26–28.

28 'Erat saeculum in quod incidit spinosis sophistarum argutiis miserrime obnoxium; inter quas tamen ille ita eluctatus est difficultates ut, si non eloquentiam profluentem illam, at neruos interim et pondus rerum sibi conquisiuerit, ac aliis tanquam per manus studiose tradiderit.' John Le-

dency to lionize every English author that preceded him, modern scholarship has not overturned his core point: William was one of the most pre-eminent teachers of his day, and though his writings are not high literature, they are evidence of creative and highly effective pedagogy.

Ex diuersis auditis is an important witness to what William passed on to his students, and to the cathedral schools in general; although there are many surviving student *reportationes* from Paris and the later universities,[29] those from cathedral schools are more scarce, and especially those recording something other than a straightforward lecture. Lincoln did not grow further into a university, and serious theological teaching seems to have come to an end there around 1225, arguably because the school failed to seize upon the opportunity to become a centre for the study of canon law;[30] clergy from the diocese in later periods received advanced theological training from other institutions.[31]

Only a handful of the poems in *Ex diuersis auditis* are attested elsewhere, mostly in William's *Versarius*; the consistency of their style makes it probable that he was responsible for most of the verses. The exception to this is the last section, 'De uoto' (55), whose mixture of rhyming schemes is more consistent with Samuel's other works. The style of the commentary in this section is outlined using schematic *distinctiones* rather than the formal prose found in the earlier sections of *Ex diuersis auditis*.[32] One also presumes that it was Samuel who

---

land, *De uiris illustribus/On Famous Men*, ed. and trans. James P. Carley, Studies and Texts 172; British Writers of the Middle Ages and the Early Modern Period 1 (Toronto and Oxford 2010), chap. 255.

29 Jacqueline Hamesse, 'La technique de la reportation,' in *L'enseignement des disciplines à la Faculté des arts (Paris et Oxford, XIIIe–XVe siècles)*, ed. Olga Weijers and Louis Holtz, Studia Artistarum 4 (Turnhout 1997), 405–421.

30 Frans van Liere, 'The Study of Canon Law and the Eclipse of the Lincoln Schools, 1175–1225,' *History of Universities* 18 (2003) 1–13.

31 F. Donald Logan, *University Education of the Parochial Clergy in Medieval England: The Lincoln Diocese, c.1300–c.1350*, Studies and Texts 188 (Toronto 2014).

32 Organization by *distinctio* was often manifested in the form of diagrams connecting various terms with lines to show their relationship. An excel-

organized the work, unless he followed the chronological order of the lessons. William favoured structures that allowed for easy reference, arranging his *Versarius* under an alphabetical scheme, and *Numerale* through a numerical plan.

Samuel follows his written sources closely in the prose to *Ex speculo cum uersibus* and *De oratione dominica*, and it is likely that he did the same in *Ex diuersis auditis*. Many of William's typical concerns are evident, and its presentation resembles William's *Distinctiones theologicae* (as found, for example, in Cambridge, Corpus Christi College, MS 186, fols 1r–20v), though it is more nuanced. The text is certainly something other than a set of notes hastily copied during a lesson or from the memory of one. It includes several passages repeated from William de Montibus's lectures on the Psalms in *Ex auditis super psalmos*. These passages are just different enough to rule out straightforward copying from the *Ex auditis super psalmos* text. His quotations of Peter Lombard, Gratian, and the *Glosa* are accurate enough to suggest that he had access to a written source. This could show that Samuel carefully assembled the contents from various sources, or even that he had a text by William from which he could copy directly; perhaps it was a mixture of both. The contents of *Ex diuersis auditis* are intellectually the work of William de Montibus, but recorded in a form reflecting the experience of Samuel Presbiter.

Goering has proposed that *Ex diuersis auditis* reflects the practice of scholastic *collationes* or *repetitiones*[33]—discourses at the end of the school day resembling a modern university seminar.[34] The verses recorded in *Ex diuersis auditis* are not

---

lent example of this method of layout translated into print is Robert Grosseteste, *Templum Dei*, ed. Joseph Goering and F.A.C. Mantello, Toronto Medieval Latin Texts 14 (Toronto 1984); on the use of the concept in the twelfth century, see Christoph H.F. Meyer, *Die Distinktionstechnik in der Kanonistik des 12. Jahrhunderts: Ein Beitrag zur Wissenschaftsgeschichte des Hochmittelalters*, Mediaevalia Lovaniensia, 1st ser., studia 29 (Leuven 2000).

33 Goering, *William de Montibus*, 504–506, with references.

34 Alexander Andrée, 'Laon Revisited: Master Anselm and the Creation of a Theological School in the Twelfth Century (A Review Essay),'

as utilitarian as some other pedagogical literature from the period, some of which cannot be understood without external texts. Some versifications of the Gospels, for instance, simply cram together relevant words and phrases into a hexameter line, and are entirely incomprehensible without knowledge of the biblical text.[35] The verses here always carry their sense independently, but cannot always stand on their own due to the use of mnemonics, explained only in the prose (as in nos 12, 16, 18, 19, 27, 30, 33, 35, 36, 44, 47, 50, 51, and 55). These are typically acronyms that form imperatives (e.g. SCOPE DOCES, 'investigate, teach,' 27.4), or sometimes nonsense words with a memorable sound (CIM CISSET NERVO, 17.1). These are often thoroughly integrated with the subject matter: SCINDE ('tear' or 'divide,' 18.3) stands for the various causes for which a marriage can be dissolved.[36] Every modern student is familiar with the sequence 'who, what, when, where, why, how': its medieval form—'quid, cui, cur, quomodo, quando, quantum' (12.8–9, literally 'what, to whom, why, how, when, how much')—is here used for remembering the purpose of works of charity.[37] Numbers are also found throughout the text as a mnemonic device, the central feature of William's *Numerale*

Journal of Medieval Latin 22 (2012) 263; Michael Clanchy and Lesley Smith, 'Abelard's Description of the School of Laon: What Might It Tell Us About Early Scholastic Teaching?,' *Nottingham Medieval Studies* 54 (2010) 19; Pierre Riché and Jacques Verger, *Des nains sur des épaules de géants: Maîtres et élèves au moyen âge* (Paris 2006), 119.

35 Greti Dinkova-Bruun, 'Remembering the Gospels in the Later Middle Ages: The Anonymous *Capitula Euangeliorum Versifice Scripta*,' *Sacris Erudiri* 48 (2009) 235–273.

36 Discussed in Greti Dinkova-Bruun, 'Notes on Poetic Composition in the Theological Schools ca. 1200 and the Latin Poetic Anthology from Ms. Harley 956: A Critical Edition,' *Sacris Erudiri* 43 (2004) 304, 320.

37 Goering, *William de Montibus*, 395 identifies some sixty uses of these words (in what he calls 'circumstantial' poems) in William de Montibus's *Versarius*; for context and use in William's *Peniteas cito*, see Marjorie Curry Woods and Rita Copeland, 'Classroom and Confession,' in *The Cambridge History of Medieval English Literature*, ed. David Wallace (Cambridge 1999), 393–394; for other variants, see D.W. Robertson Jr, 'A Note on the Classical Origin of "Circumstances" in the Medieval Confessional,' *Studies in Philology* 43.1 (1946) 6–14.

and a practice that would become even more common in his later writings.[38]

Ex diuersis auditis originated in a crucial period for the development of *pastoralia*, as Leonard Boyle called the literature of pastoral care, identifying a movement to create accessible manuals for the purpose, beginning between the Third and Fourth Lateran Councils of 1179 and 1215.[39] There is a great deal of interest in the priest's role as a member of the community, promoting good character and judgement (see especially nos 2, 4, 24, 25) and exceptional preaching (the topic that prompts the longest analysis in the work, no. 39). This reflects William de Montibus's concern to transform theories into principles, shared by contemporaries such as Peter the Chanter and Alan of Lille.[40] Another of William's students, Richard of Wetheringsett, has a similar focus in his *summa* known from its incipit as *Qui bene presunt.*[41]

The Manuscript

The manuscript of *Ex diuersis auditis*, Oxford, Bodleian Library, MS Bodley 860 (*SC* 2723), is written entirely in Latin, with pages measuring around 200 × 270 mm. It is composite,

38 Further references in M.B. Parkes, '*Folia librorum quaerere:* Medieval Experience of the Problems of Hypertext and the Index,' in *Fabula in tabula: Una storia degli indici dal manoscritto al testo elettronico*, ed. Claudio Leonardi, Quaderni di cultura mediolatina 13 (Spoleto 1995), 34 nn 41–44.

39 Joseph Goering, 'Leonard E. Boyle and the Invention of *Pastoralia*,' in *A Companion to Pastoral Care in the Late Middle Ages (1200–1500)*, ed. Ronald J. Stansbury, Brill's Companions to the Christian Tradition 22 (Leiden 2010), 7–20; Leonard E. Boyle, 'The Inter-Conciliar Period 1179–1215 and the Beginnings of Pastoral Manuals,' in *Miscellanea Rolando Bandinelli, Papa Alessandro III*, ed. Filippo Liotta (Siena 1986), 45–56.

40 Albrecht Diem, 'Virtues and Vices in Early Texts on Pastoral Care,' *Franciscan Studies* 62 (2004) 193–223.

41 Joseph Goering, 'The Summa *Qui bene presunt* and Its Author,' in *Literature and Religion in the Later Middle Ages: Philological Studies in Honor of Siegfried Wenzel*, ed. Richard G. Newhauser and John A. Alford, Medieval and Renaissance Texts and Studies 118 (Binghampton, NY 1995), 143–159.

consisting of three separate booklets,[42] collated i, 1^8 | 2^8–6^8, 7^{8-3} (6/7/8 canc.), 8^8–12^8 | 13^8–24^8, 25^{8+2} (4/5 add.), 26^8, i. A note on the flyleaf in the hand of librarian Henry Kirkestede (ca. 1314–ca. 1378) testifies that it belonged to the abbey of Bury St Edmunds:

> Liber monachorum sancti Edmundi in quo continentur
> Postille seu collecta super psalterium
> in scolis magistri G. de montibus
> Collecta samuelis presbiteri in scolis predictis

A pressmark of B. 233 is also from the abbey library; B. 231, B. 232, and B. 240 also survive in modern libraries, all containing commentaries on the Psalms.[43] It is written and decorated in a similar style to some other Bury manuscripts, and may have been produced there.[44] The book was among others from Bury bequeathed to Pembroke College by William Smart in 1599;[45] Thomas James lists it there in his survey of Oxford and Cambridge libraries,[46] but it is one of thirty-one manuscripts separated from the Pembroke collection, with several of them now in Oxford.[47] The *Summary Catalogue* con-

42 For an explanation of this concept, see Alexandra Gillespie, 'Medieval Books, Their Booklets, and Booklet Theory,' *English Manuscript Studies 1100–1700* 16 (2011) 1–29.

43 Richard Sharpe, 'Reconstructing the Medieval Library of Bury St Edmunds Abbey: The Lost Catalogue of Henry of Kirkstead,' in *Bury St Edmunds: Medieval Art, Architecture, Archaeology, and Economy*, ed. Antonia Gransden, Conference Transactions 20 (Leeds 1998), 210, categorizes these under a larger 'Biblia' section; for an earlier listing, see M.R. James, 'Bury St. Edmunds Manuscripts,' *English Historical Review* 41.162 (1926) 254.

44 Cf. Cambridge, Pembroke College, MS 54: Gransden, *History of the Abbey of Bury St Edmunds*, plate 10, reproduces the first folio.

45 M.R. James, *On the Abbey of S. Edmund at Bury* (Cambridge 1895), 15–16, prints Matthew Wren's list; for a summary of the Bury library's history, see Sharpe et al., *English Benedictine Libraries*, 43–49.

46 Thomas James, *Ecloga Oxonio-Cantabrigiensis* (London 1600), 2:132 (no. 149).

47 Listed in M.R. James and Ellis H. Minns, *A Descriptive Catalogue of the Manuscripts in the Library of Pembroke College, Cambridge* (Cambridge 1905), xx–xxiii, where this manuscript is no. 2077; this follows its enumeration in Edward Bernard, *Catalogi librorum manuscriptorum Angliæ*

jectures that the Bodleian Library acquired the book in 1603 or 1604.

The scribe of *Ex diuersis auditis* was not always able to read the exemplar, but sought to copy it precisely without intervening in the text. In particular, the scribe often writes 'c' or 't' for 'm' and 'n' (resulting, for example, in 'acumaretur' for 'animaretur,' 'iutibra' for 'umbra,' 'consideratis' for 'considerans,' 'sitium' for 'sinum') and for 'r' ('tectum' for 'rectum,' 'iurate' for 'iurare,' 'considerate' for 'considerare,' 'carhalogus' for 'cathalogus,' 'fiete' for 'fieri'; in reverse, 'ira' for 'ita'). There are also some lacunae, later filled in by a corrector whose hand appears throughout the Samuel Presbiter manuscripts; a faint note in the lower corner of fol. 103r, 'usque hunc in parte,' suggests that he worked through the texts methodically. Some of the alterations are so obvious that any intelligent reader might have made them, but others seem to be original, in particular the five points in the text where the corrector adds a variant for understanding the verse (e.g. *uel legit* for *posuit*, 5.3), a device found throughout Samuel's works. These are usually unmetrical, and not emendations to the original verse (which the corrector does not hesitate to execute, especially later in the manuscript for *Ad habendam memoriam*). There are also cases in which the corrector appears to be revising the work rather than replicating the exemplar, as when he changes 'multi' to 'pharisei' to match the Vulgate at 25.19, or when he changes 'quia' to 'que' at 39.46. He also carefully revises the punctuation, particularly adding more *puncti eleuati* to the verses. It seems plausible that this corrector is Samuel himself.

Sources

The work uses biblical texts as the basis for most of its arguments, making frequent use of allegorical interpretations. As is typical in this period, it introduces the majority of quotations

---

et Hiberniæ in unum collecti (Oxford 1697), which for Pembroke simply reprints the listing in James, *Ecloga*.

only by a generic phrase such as 'dicitur' or 'unde illud' (if it signals them at all), and the text can vary wildly at times from any identifiable variant of the Vulgate, indicating that they are either quoted from memory or via another source.[48] It treats biblical sources in a fluid way to suit a particular didactic purpose, for example in combining quotations from non-contiguous passages without any sign for the reader.

There are also quotations from classical authors (Juvenal, Ovid, Horace), never by name, but often conventionally identified as a 'poeta.' There are also some references to the liturgy ('in oratione'). It cites only one medieval author (Pope Alexander) by name, but identifies patristic sources explicitly (Jerome, Augustine, Gregory the Great, Chrysostom, Isidore, Origen). These are generally quoted via a more recent source, such as Peter Lombard's *Sentences*, the classic medieval textbook on theology from the twelfth century;[49] and from its peer in canon law, Gratian's *Decretum*.[50] Etymologies are often drawn from the marginal and interlinear *Glosa* (as 55.42 refers to it), later known as the *Glossa ordinaria* to the Bible, though its precise influence is difficult to pin down due to the lack of an edition representative of the version William or Samuel might have used.[51]

48 The edited text generally follows Robert Weber et al., eds, *Biblia Sacra iuxta vulgatam versionem*, 5th ed. (Stuttgart 2007); I have not reported variants found either in this edition or the larger ones it employs: for the Old Testament, *Biblia Sacra iuxta latinam vulgatam versionem ad codicum fidem* (Rome 1926–1995); and for the New Testament, *Nouum Testamentum Domini nostri Iesu Christi Latine, secundum editionem sancti Hieronymi*, ed. John Wordsworth and Henry Julian White (Oxford 1889–1954).

49 On the educational use of this book, see Ricardo Saccenti, 'Questions et Sentences: L'enseignement entre la fin du XIIe et le début du XIIIe siècle,' in *Les débuts de l'enseignement universitaire à Paris (1200–1245 environ)*, ed. Jacques Verger and Olga Weijers, Studia Artistarum 38 (Turnhout 2013), 275–293.

50 For an introduction to Gratian, see Anders Winroth, *The Making of Gratian's* Decretum, Cambridge Studies in Medieval Life and Thought, 4th ser., 49 (Cambridge 2000), chap. 1.

51 Margaret T. Gibson, 'The Twelfth-Century Glossed Bible,' in *Papers Presented to the Tenth International Conference on Patristic Studies Held in*

Ex diuersis auditis has many parallels with Peter the Chanter's *Verbum adbreuiatum* and *Summa de sacramentis et animae consiliis*, but these appear to reflect the teachers' shared milieu rather than direct use of either of these works. After R.W. Hunt suggested a link between the figures, Hugh MacKinnon argued that Peter the Chanter was a teacher of William de Montibus;[52] Goering found the evidence for this to be unsustainable, while allowing that they might have known one another.[53] The most recent editor of the *Verbum adbreuiatum* dates the short version of the work to 1187–1191, the *Summa de sacramentis* to 1191–1192, and the later versions of the *Verbum adbreuiatum* to after Peter's death in 1197.[54] William de Montibus could not have seen them in Paris, but a copy of the *Verbum adbreuiatum* was probably available in Lincoln during his time, as the *Gemma ecclesiastica*, which Gerald of Wales wrote while he was studying in Lincoln around 1196–1199,[55] is heavily dependent on this book.[56] Gerald uses the short version now published as the

---

Oxford, 1987, ed. E.A. Livingstone, vol. 5, Studia Patristica 23 (Leuven 1989), 243 also notes its use in *Ex auditis super psalmos*.

52 R.W. Hunt, 'English Learning in the Late Twelfth Century,' *Transactions of the Royal Historical Society*, 4th ser., 19 (1936) 21; Hugh MacKinnon, 'William de Montibus: A Medieval Teacher,' in *Essays in Medieval History Presented to Bertie Wilkinson*, ed. T.A. Sandquist and M.R. Powicke (Toronto 1968), 33.

53 Goering, *William de Montibus*, 11–12.

54 For a summary of her arguments and an alternate view, see John W. Baldwin, 'An Edition of the Long Version of Peter the Chanter's *Verbum Abbreviatum*,' *Journal of Ecclesiastical History* 57.1 (2006) 78–85.

55 James F. Dimock, introduction to Gerald of Wales, *Topographia Hibernica et Expugnatio Hibernica*, vol. 5 of *Giraldi Cambrensis opera*, ed. James F. Dimock, Rolls Series 21 (London 1867), liii n. 2; cited with further context in Brian Golding, 'Gerald of Wales, the *Gemma Ecclesiastica* and Pastoral Care,' in *Text and Traditions of Medieval Pastoral Care: Essays in Honour of Bella Millett*, ed. Cate Gunn and Catherine Innes-Parker (Woodbridge, Suffolk 2009), 48, 51.

56 André Boutemy, 'Giraud de Barri et Pierre le Chantre: Une source de la *Gemma ecclesiastica*,' *Revue du moyen âge latin* 2 (1946) 45–62; E.M. Sanford, 'Giraldus Cambrensis' Debt to Petrus Cantor,' *Medievalia et Humanistica* 3 (1945) 16–32; Golding, 'Gerald of Wales,' 52–54.

textus prior,[57] but *Ex diuersis auditis* has parallels in all three versions, with the least correlation to the *textus prior*. The resemblances to Peter the Chanter's works in *Ex diuersis auditis* sometimes consist of nothing more than a similarity of unusual vocabulary or a kindred strain of ideas. There is also much relevant discourse in Peter's works that is not used: in some cases, a section in *Ex diuersis auditis* with a title identical to a chapter of the *Verbum adbreuiatum* takes a divergent approach to the subject. Despite the number of similarities, one cannot here identify direct use of Peter the Chanter's works.

Though there is little direct evidence for the later use of *Ex diuersis auditis*, it includes several passages that resemble later works written by Peter the Chanter's students, notably those by Thomas of Chobham,[58] which appear without any known parallel in earlier scholastic works. One must be cautious about drawing inferences from this, as there are even certain passages in *Ex diuersis auditis* that have more in common with Bonaventure or Thomas Aquinas than works contemporary with William de Montibus, indicating the continuity of the oral scholastic tradition, and reflecting the number of sources from this period still left unpublished.

Metre and Rhyme

The verses use a combination of simple Leonines and *elegi Leonini*, which consist respectively of classical hexameters and elegiac couplets, with the addition of a rhyme between the

57 See for instance *Gemma ecclesiastica* 2.26 in Boutemy, 'Giraud de Barri et Pierre le Chantre,' 49; this is only found in Peter the Chanter, *Verbum adbreuiatum: Textus prior*, ed. Monique Boutry, CCCM 196a (Turnhout 2012), chap. 22 (pp 175–176, lines 71–90), which is much closer to Gerald's text than the version Boutemy cites: Peter the Chanter, *Verbum abbreuiatum, opus morale*, ed. Georges Galopin (Mons: Waudré, 1639; repr. 1855, in PL 205:21–554).

58 On their relationship, see John W. Baldwin, *Masters, Princes, and Merchants: The Social Views of Peter the Chanter and His Circle* (Princeton 1970), 1:34–36.

caesura (always occurring in the third foot) and the end of the line.[59] Written fluidly with relatively few syntactical contortions, these admirably achieve their purpose of functioning as a memory aid.

Written in Leonines are 2, 3, 4, 7, 16, 18–20, 22–25, 27–35, and 37–54. Written in *elegi Leonini* are 1, 5, 6, 8–15, 17, 21, 26, and 36. The first two verses of no. 2 omit the rhyme, though the second of these adapts the penultimate verse of 37, which includes it. The last section, 55, is in hexameter, but uses an inconsistent scheme for its rhymes, and its commentary is also of a different character from the work. It uses Leonines for the first and fourth verses; verses two and three are *collaterales* (with the last syllable before the caesura rhyming with the successive caesura, and likewise for the end of each line); verse five is unrhymed. This mixture is also found in Samuel's versification of Psalm 1,[60] and it seems likely that Samuel himself wrote it rather than William de Montibus.

Most of the rhymes are monosyllabic (5.3–4, forming an elegiac couplet):

īntēr | sūr cā|*dēs* · ăbră|hām pŏsŭ|īt sĭbĭ | sē*des*
crīmĕn ĭn | hīs dē|l*ēt* · uīr bŏnŭ|s ātquĕ că|u*et*

There are also many disyllabic rhymes (19.2–3, in hexameter):

sī mălĕ | iū*rān*|*dī* · fōr|mās sīt | mēns mĕmŏ|*rāndi*
pēr prī|mās f*ā*|*tō* · pĕr ĭ|dōnĕă | cōmmĕmŏ|r*āto*

Some of the lines hardly fit the modern definition of a rhyme (2.6):

sēx īs|tīs uēr|bīs · nŏtĕt | ēssĕ tĕ|nēndă să|cērdos

In most cases, the scheme is consistently applied. Occasionally one must know the intended sound for individual letters, as in this verse (30.3):

59 For an introduction to metre in this period, see A.G. Rigg, *A History of Anglo-Latin Literature, 1066–1422* (Cambridge 1992), 313–329, with examples of Leonines at 319 and of *elegi Leonini* at 322.

60 Dinkova-Bruun, 'Samuel Presbyter,' 156.

quōd dē|sīgnāt | c[*ē*] · gĕnĕr|ālĕ uĕl | ēst spĕcĭ|āl*e*

Verses such as this can be easily understood as long as one keeps in mind the differences between classical and medieval pronunciation, remembering at 42.2, for instance, that 'caus*e*' rhymes with 'tacer*e*.'[61]

Editorial Practice

Ex diuersis auditis is here edited in its entirety for the first time; Goering printed the first section alongside the headings and first lines for the rest.[62] My numbering differs from his (1–55 rather than 1–54), as I have split no. 16 into two parts. Sections that overlap with *Versarius* have been compared with Cambridge, Corpus Christi College, MS 186, resulting in one emendation (at 4.6); other variants are not reported.

The layout of the text as presented here does not reproduce the manuscript, presenting it instead using print conventions. As a result of these interventions, folio references can only specify the location of verses. The original begins with commentary rather than the verses, with individual lines of poetry copied underneath the relevant prose passage. The scribe shows the relationship of longer passages to their lines only through placement on the page, while shorter ones have a wavy line drawn to the word to which they apply. The edited text uses a combination of line numbers (referring to the verse lines) and lemmata indicating the relevant passage where necessary; this is generally applied only to those passages specifically linked using a line in the manuscript. While the references in the commentary are not entirely the result of editorial interpretation, readers

61 For general guidance, see A.G. Rigg, 'Anglo-Latin,' in *Singing Early Music: The Pronunciation of European Languages in the Late Middle Ages and Renaissance*, ed. Timothy J. McGee (Bloomington 1996), 46–61.

62 Goering, *William de Montibus*, 508–514; the text was also briefly described in Beryl Smalley and George Lacombe, 'The Lombard's Commentary on Isaias and Other Fragments,' *The New Scholasticism* 5.2 (1931) 141–142.

should not surmise that the original is more precise than it truly is.

In the manuscript, the mnemonic acronyms used at several points in the commentary are only written out in the verse, using wider spacing to fit in the words above, and joining each letter by an individual line to its matching word. I have instead written the mnemonic in small capitals in the verse, and repeated the letters beside the words to which they apply. The commentary for the last section in the work (no. 55) is arranged using *distinctiones*, and translates poorly onto a small printed page. The edited text follows the form of an outline, in which each item higher in the hierarchy applies to the subordinate items; this does not entail rearrangement of the text.

The critical apparatus records the alterations to the manuscript and editorial changes, referring to the corrector as 'another hand.' The text reproduces the spelling of the manuscript, even in its inconsistencies. The scribe uses 'ci' and 'ti' with particular irregularity; one finds, for instance, 'iuditio' at 12.21 but 'iudicium' at 12.30, or 'ociose' incompletely changed to 'otiose' in 19.28. The scribe never writes 'Christus' or 'Cristus' in an unabbreviated form, but some contemporary English manuscripts use the latter form; 'Cristiani' (30.8), 'Crisostomus' (51.8), and 'crisma' (26.7) suggest the spelling without an 'h.'[63] Minuscule 'v' occurs only decoratively in the manuscript, in both an initial and medial position, and without any consistency; the edition makes no distinction between 'u' and 'v,' using 'V' in the majuscule. The manuscript influences the punctuation as printed, but it has been freely adapted.

The commentary seeks to show sources and parallels for the text and assist students of medieval Latin, glossing words with particularly troublesome spellings in their classical form, and providing definitions for unusual words whose meaning might not be quickly guessed. For other vocabulary, readers will receive the best guidance from the *Dictionary of Medieval Latin*

63 Cf. Peter Stotz, *Handbuch zur lateinischen Sprache des Mittelalters*, Handbuch der Altertumswissenschaft, 2.5 (Munich 1996–2004), 3:168 (VII § 128.3).

from British Sources, to which the commentary refers where it includes quotations helpful in illustrating the contemporary usage of a word or phrase.

BIBLIOGRAPHY

Adam of St Victor. *Les séquences d'Adam de Saint-Victor: Étude littéraire (poétique et rhétorique), textes et traductions, commentaires*. Ed. and trans. Jean Grosfillier. Bibliotheca Victorina 20 (Turnhout 2008).

Alexander Neckam. *De naturis rerum libri duo. With the poem of the same author, De laudibus divinæ sapientiæ*. Ed. Thomas Wright. Rolls Series 34 (London 1863).

——. *Sacerdos ad altare*. Ed. Christopher J. McDonough. CCCM 227 (Turnhout 2010).

Alexander of Hales. *Glossa in quatuor libros Sententiarum Petri Lombardi*. Bibliotheca franciscana scholastica medii aevi 12–15. (Quaracchi, Florence 1951).

——. *Summa theologica* (Quaracchi, Florence 1924–1948).

Ambrose. *De officiis*. Ed. Maurice Testard. CCSL 15 (Turnhout 2000).

Andrée, Alexander. 'Laon Revisited: Master Anselm and the Creation of a Theological School in the Twelfth Century (A Review Essay).' *Journal of Medieval Latin* 22 (2012) 257–281.

Aristotle. *Topica: Translatio Boethii, fragmentum recensionis alterius et translatio anonyma*. Ed. Laurent Minio-Paluello. Aristoteles Latinus 5.1–3 (Brussels 1969).

Augustine. *Epistulae*. Ed. Klaus D. Daur. CCSL 31, 31a, 31b (Turnhout 2004–2009).

——. *Sermones selecti duodeuiginti*. Ed. Cyrille Lambot. Stromata patristica et mediaevalia 1 (Brussels 1950).

Baldwin, John W. 'An Edition of the Long Version of Peter the Chanter's *Verbum Abbreviatum*.' *Journal of Ecclesiastical History* 57.1 (2006) 78–85.

——. *Masters, Princes, and Merchants: The Social Views of Peter the Chanter and His Circle* (Princeton 1970).

Bede. 'De tabernaculo et uasis eius ac uestibus sacerdotum libri III.' In *Opera exegetica*, ed. David Hurst 2.2a, pp 5–139. CCSL 119a (Turnhout 1969).

Bernard, Edward. *Catalogi librorum manuscriptorum Angliæ et Hiberniæ in unum collecti* (Oxford 1697).

Bernard of Clairvaux. *Sermones*. Ed. Jean Leclercq and H.M. Rochais. Sancti Bernardi opera 4–6 (Rome 1966–1972).

——. *Sermones super Cantica Canticorum*. Ed. Jean Leclercq, C.H. Talbot, and H.M. Rochais. Sancti Bernardi opera 1–2 (Rome 1957–1958).

[Bible.] *Biblia latina cum glossa ordinaria: Facsimile reprint of the editio princeps, Adolph Rusch of Strassburg 1480/81*. Ed. Margaret T. Gibson and Karlfried Froehlich (Turnhout 1992).

——. *Biblia Sacra iuxta Vulgatam versionem*. Ed. Robert Weber, Bonifatius Fischer, Jean Gribomount, Hedley F.D. Sparks, Walter Thiele, and Roger Gryson. 5th ed. (Stuttgart 2007).

——. *Biblia Sacra iuxta Latinam Vulgatam versionem ad codicum fidem*; iussu Pii pp. XI, cura et studio monachorum Sancti Benedicti Commissionis Pontificiae a Pio X institutae sodalium praeside Aidano Gasquet, cardinale edita (Rome 1926–1995).

——. *Nouum Testamentum Domini nostri Iesu Christi Latine, secundum editionem sancti Hieronymi*. Ed. John Wordsworth and Henry Julian White (Oxford 1889–1954).

Boutemy, André. 'Giraud de Barri et Pierre le Chantre: Une source de la *Gemma ecclesiastica*.' *Revue du moyen âge latin* 2 (1946) 45–62.

Boyle, Leonard E. 'The Inter-Conciliar Period 1179–1215 and the Beginnings of Pastoral Manuals.' In *Miscellanea Rolando Bandinelli, Papa Alessandro III*, ed. Filippo Liotta, pp 45–56 (Siena 1986).

Brundage, James A. 'Marriage and Sexuality in the Decretals of Pope Alexander III.' In *Miscellanea Rolando Bandinelli, Papa Alessandro III*, ed. Filippo Liotta, pp 57–83 (Siena 1986).

——. *Medieval Canon Law and the Crusader* (Madison 1969).

Carruthers, Mary J. *The Book of Memory: A Study of Memory in Medieval Culture*. 2nd ed. Cambridge Studies in Medieval Literature 10 (Cambridge 2008).

Cassiodorus. *Expositio Psalmorum*. Ed. Marc Adriaen. CCSL 97–98 (Turnhout 1958).

Clanchy, Michael and Lesley Smith. 'Abelard's Description of the School of Laon: What Might It Tell Us About Early Scholastic Teaching?' *Nottingham Medieval Studies* 54 (2010) 1–34.

Curry Woods, Marjorie and Rita Copeland. 'Classroom and Confession.' In *The Cambridge History of Medieval English Literature*, ed. David Wallace, pp 376–406 (Cambridge 1999).

Deshusses, Jean, ed. *Le sacramentaire grégorien: Ses principales formes d'après les plus anciens manuscrits*. Spicilegum friburgense 16, 24, 28 (Fribourg 1971).

Diem, Albrecht. 'Virtues and Vices in Early Texts on Pastoral Care.' *Franciscan Studies* 62 (2004) 193–223.

Dines, Ilya. 'The Earliest Use of John of Salisbury's *Policraticus*: Third Family Bestiaries.' *Viator* 44.1 (2013) 107–118.

Dinkova-Bruun, Greti. 'Biblical Versifications from Late Antiquity to the Middle of the Thirteenth Century: History or Allegory?' In *Poetry and Exegesis in Premodern Latin Christianity: The Encounter Between Classical and Christian Strategies of Interpretation*, ed. Willemien Otten and Karla Pollmann, pp 315–342. Supplements to *Vigiliae Christianae* 87 (Leiden 2007).

——. 'Notes on Poetic Composition in the Theological Schools ca. 1200 and the Latin Poetic Anthology from Ms. Harley 956: A Critical Edition.' *Sacris Erudiri* 43 (2004) 299–391.

——. 'Remembering the Gospels in the Later Middle Ages: The Anonymous *Capitula Euangeliorum Versifice Scripta*.' *Sacris Erudiri* 48 (2009) 235–273.

——. 'Samuel Presbyter and the Glosses to His Versification of Psalm 1: An Anti-Church Invective?' In *Florilegium mediaevale: Études offertes à Jacqueline Hamesse à l'occasion de son éméritat*, ed. José Francisco Meirinhos and Olga Weijers, p 155–174. Textes et études du moyen âge 50 (Louvain-la-Neuve 2009).

——. 'The Verse Bible as Aide-Mémoire.' In *The Making of Memory in the Middle Ages*, ed. Lucie Doležalová, pp 115–131. Later Medieval Europe 4 (Leiden 2010).

Foster, C.W. and Kathleen Major, eds. *The Registrum Antiquissimum of the Cathedral Church of Lincoln*. Publications of the Lincoln Record Society 27–29, 32, 34, 41, 42, 46, 51, 62, 67, 68 (Hereford 1931–1973).

Friedberg, Emil, ed. *Corpus iuris canonici* (2nd ed, Leipzig 1879–1881).

Gerald of Wales. *Gemma ecclesiastica,* vol. 2 of *Giraldi Cambrensis opera.* Ed. J.S. Brewer. Rolls Series 21 (London 1862).

——. *Speculum ecclesiae,* vol. 4 of *Giraldi Cambrensis opera.* Ed. J.S. Brewer. Rolls Series 21 (London 1873).

——. *Topographia Hibernica et Expugnatio Hibernica,* vol. 5 of *Giraldi Cambrensis opera.* Ed. James F. Dimock. Rolls Series 21 (London 1867).

——. 'Vita S. Hugonis.' In *Giraldi Cambrensis Opera* 7, ed. James F. Dimock, pp 81–147. Rolls Series 21 (London 1877).

Gibson, Margaret T. 'The Twelfth-Century Glossed Bible.' In *Papers Presented to the Tenth International Conference on Patristic Studies Held in Oxford, 1987* 5, ed. E.A. Livingstone, pp 232–244. Studia Patristica 23 (Leuven 1989).

Gilbert de la Porrée. *The Commentaries on Boethius*. Ed. Nikolaus M. Häring. Studies and Texts 13 (Toronto 1966).

Gillespie, Alexandra. 'Medieval Books, Their Booklets, and Booklet Theory.' *English Manuscript Studies 1100–1700* 16 (2011) 1–29.

Goering, Joseph. 'Leonard E. Boyle and the Invention of *Pastoralia.*' In *A Companion to Pastoral Care in the Late Middle Ages (1200–1500)*, ed. Ronald J. Stansbury, pp 7–20. Brill's Companions to the Christian Tradition 22 (Leiden 2010).

——. 'The Summa *Qui bene presunt* and Its Author.' In *Literature and Religion in the Later Middle Ages: Philological Studies in Honor of Siegfried Wenzel*, ed. Richard G. Newhauser and John A. Alford, pp 143–159. Medieval and Renaissance Texts and Studies 118 (Binghampton, NY 1995).

——. *William de Montibus (c. 1140–1213): The Schools and the Literature of Pastoral Care*. Studies and Texts 108 (Toronto 1992).

Golding, Brian. 'Gerald of Wales, the *Gemma Ecclesiastica* and Pastoral Care.' In *Text and Traditions of Medieval Pastoral Care: Essays in Honour of Bella Millett*, ed. Cate Gunn and Catherine Innes-Parker, pp 47–61 (Woodbridge, Suffolk 2009).

Gransden, Antonia. *A History of the Abbey of Bury St Edmunds, 1182–1256: Samson of Tottington to Edmund of Walpole*. Studies in the History of Medieval Religion 31 (Woodbridge, Suffolk 2007).

Gregory the Great. *Moralia in Iob*. Ed. Marc Adriaen. CCSL 143, 143a, 143b (Turnhout 1979–1985).

Guillaume Durand. *Rationale divinorum officiorum*. Ed. A. Davril and T.M. Thibodeau. CCCM 140, 140a, 140b (Turnhout 1995–2013).

Hamesse, Jacqueline. 'La technique de la reportation.' In *L'enseignement des disciplines à la Faculté des arts (Paris et Oxford, XIIIe–XVe siècles)*, ed. Olga Weijers and Louis Holtz, pp 405–421. Studia Artistarum 4 (Turnhout 1997).

Harper-Bill, Christopher, ed. *Dodnash Priory Charters*. Suffolk Charters 16 (Woodbridge, Suffolk 1998).

Heiric of Auxerre. *Homiliae per circulum anni*. Ed. Richard Quadri. CCCM 116, 116a, 116b (Turnhout 1992–1994).

Horace. *Opera*. Ed. Friedrich Klinger. Bibliotheca Teubneriana 1225. 3rd ed. (Leipzig 1959).

Hugh of Fouilloy. *The Medieval Book of Birds: Hugh of Fouilloy's* Aviarium. Ed. and trans. Willene B. Clark. Medieval and Renaissance Texts and Studies 80 (Binghamton, NY 1992).

Hunt, R.W. 'English Learning in the Late Twelfth Century.' *Transactions of the Royal Historical Society*, 4th ser., 19 (1936) 19–42.

——. 'The Collections of a Monk of Bardney: A Dismembered Rawlinson Manuscript (MSS. Rawl. C. 502 + C. 510 + D. 893, fol. 19–26, 105–6, 113).' *Mediaeval and Renaissance Studies* 5 (1961) 28–42.

James, M.R. 'Bury St. Edmunds Manuscripts.' *English Historical Review* 41.162 (1926) 251–260.

——. *On the Abbey of S. Edmund at Bury* (Cambridge 1895).

James, M.R. and Ellis H. Minns. *A Descriptive Catalogue of the Manuscripts in the Library of Pembroke College, Cambridge* (Cambridge 1905).

James, Thomas. *Ecloga Oxonio-Cantabrigiensis* (London 1600).

Jerome. *Commentariorum in Matheum libri IV*. Ed. David Hurst and Marc Adriaen. CCSL 77 (Turnhout 1969).

——. *Epistulae*. Ed. Isidorus Hilberg. CSEL 54, 55, 56 (Vienna 1910–1918).

——. 'Liber interpretationis hebraicorum nominum.' In *S. Hieronymi presbyteri opera*, ed. Paul de Lagarde, pp 59–161. Vol 1.1. CCSL 72 (Turnhout 1959).

——. 'Tractatus siue homiliae in psalmos.' In *S. Hieronymi Presbyteri Opera*, ed. Germain Morin, pp 1–352. Vol 2.2. CCSL 78 (Turnhout 1958).

John of Salisbury. *Policratici siue De nugis curialium et uestigiis philosophorum libri VIII*. Ed. Clement C.J. Webb (Oxford 1909).

Kuttner, Stephan and Eleanor Rathbone. 'Anglo-Norman Canonists of the Twelfth Century: An Introductory Study.' *Traditio* 7 (1949–1951) 279–358.

Law, Vivien. 'Why Write a Verse Grammar?' *Journal of Medieval Latin* 9 (1999) 46–76.

Leland, John. *De uiris illustribus/On Famous Men*. Ed. and trans. James P. Carley. Studies and Texts 172; British Writers of the Middle Ages and the Early Modern Period 1 (Toronto and Oxford 2010).

Logan, F. Donald. *University Education of the Parochial Clergy in Medieval England: The Lincoln Diocese, c.1300–c.1350*. Studies and Texts 188 (Toronto 2014).

Lombardo, Eleonora. 'Ecclesia huius temporis: La Chiesa militante nelle prime raccolte dei sermoni dei frati minori (1225ca–1260).' (PhD thesis, Università di Padova, 2010).

MacKinnon, Hugh. 'William de Montibus: A Medieval Teacher.' In *Essays in Medieval History Presented to Bertie Wilkinson*, ed. T.A. Sandquist and M.R. Powicke, pp 32–45 (Toronto 1968).

Meyer, Christoph H.F. *Die Distinktionstechnik in der Kanonistik des 12. Jahrhunderts: Ein Beitrag zur Wissenschaftsgeschichte des Hochmittelalters*. Mediaevalia Lovaniensia,

1st ser., studia 29 (Leuven 2000).

Morgan, Nigel J. *Early Gothic Manuscripts*. Survey of Manuscripts Illuminated in the British Isles 4 (London 1982–1988).

——. *The Lambeth Apocalypse, Manuscript 209 in Lambeth Palace Library: A Critical Study* (London 1990).

Notker Balbulus. 'Liber ymnorum.' In *Notker der Dichter und seine geistige Welt*, ed. Wolfram von den Steinen. Vol. 2. 2nd ed (Bern 1978).

Origen. *Origenes Werke VI. Homilien zum Hexateuch in Rufins Übersetzung. Teil 1: Die Homilien zu Genesis (Homiliae in Genesin)*. Ed. Peter Habermehl. Die griechischen christlichen Schriftsteller der ersten Jahrhunderte, n.s., 17. 2nd ed. (Berlin 2012).

——. *Origenes Werke VI. Homilien zum Hexateuch in Rufins Übersetzung. Teil 1: Die Homilien zu Genesis, Exodus und Leviticus*. Ed. Wilhelm Adolf Baehrens. Die griechischen christlichen Schriftsteller der ersten Jahrhunderte 29 (Leipzig 1920).

——. *Origenes Werke VII. Homilien zum Hexateuch in Rufins Übersetzung. Teil 2: Die Homilien zu Numeri, Josua und Judices*. Ed. Wilhelm Adolf Baehrens. Die griechischen christlichen Schriftsteller der ersten Jahrhunderte 30 (Leipzig 1921).

Ovid. *Metamorphoses*. Ed. R.J. Tarrant. Oxford Classical Texts (Oxford 2004).

Parkes, M.B. '*Folia librorum quaerere:* Medieval Experience of the Problems of Hypertext and the Index.' In *Fabula in tabula: Una storia degli indici dal manoscritto al testo elettronico*, ed. Claudio Leonardi, pp 23–41. Quaderni di cultura mediolatina 13 (Spoleto 1995).

Peter Abelard. 'Theologia christiana.' In *Opera theologica*, ed. E.M. Buytaert, pp 71–372. Vol. 2. CCCM 12 (Turnhout 1969).

Peter Comestor. *Historia scholastica: Opus eximium magnam sacræ Scripturæ partem, quae et in Serie, et in Glossis crebro diffusa erat, breviter complectens*. Ed. Emanuel Navarrus (Madrid 1699; repr. 1855 in PL 198:1049–1722).

——. *Scolastica historia: Liber Genesis*. Ed. Agneta Sylwan. CCCM 191 (Turnhout 2005).

Peter Lombard. *In omnes D. Pauli Apost. Epistolas Collectanea* (Paris 1535; repr. 1854 in PL 191:1297–1696, 192:9–520).

——. *In totum psalterium eximii prophetarum Dauid commentarii*. Ed. Richard of Le Mans (Paris 1541; repr. 1854 in PL 191:31–1296).

——. *Sententiae in IV libris distinctae*. Ed. Ignatius F. Brady. Spicilegium Bonaventurianum 4–5. 3rd ed. (Grottaferrata 1971–1981).

Peter of Blois. *Carmina*. Ed. Carsten Wollin. CCCM 128 (Turnhout 1998).

Peter of Poitiers. *Summa de confessione: Compilatio praesens*. Ed. Jean Longère. CCCM 51 (Turnhout 1980).

Peter the Chanter. *Summa de sacramentis et animae consiliis*. Ed. Jean-Albert Dugauquier. Analecta mediaevalia Namurcensia 4, 7, 11, 16, 21 (Leuven 1954–1967).

——. *Verbum abbreuiatum, opus morale*. Ed. Georges Galopin (Mons 1639; repr. 1855 in PL 205:21–554).

——. *Verbum adbreuiatum: Textus alter*. Ed. Monique Boutry. CCCM 196b (Turnhout 2012).

——. *Verbum adbreuiatum: Textus conflatus*. Ed. Monique Boutry. CCCM 196 (Turnhout 2004).

——. *Verbum adbreuiatum: Textus prior*. Ed. Monique Boutry. CCCM 196a (Turnhout 2012).

Peter the Venerable. *The Letters of Peter the Venerable*. Ed. Giles Constable. Harvard Historical Studies 78 (Cambridge, MA 1967).

Pipe Roll Society, Great Britain, ed. *Feet of Fines of the Tenth Year of the Reign of King Richard I, AD 1198 to AD 1199*. Publications of the Pipe Roll Society 24 (London 1900).

Pompeius. 'Commentum artis Donati.' In *Artium scriptores minores*, ed. Heinrich Keil, pp 81–312. Grammatici Latini 5 (Leipzig 1868).

Riché, Pierre and Jacques Verger. *Des nains sur des épaules de géants: Maîtres et élèves au moyen âge* (Paris 2006).

Rigg, A.G. *A History of Anglo-Latin Literature, 1066–1422* (Cambridge 1992).

——. 'Anglo-Latin.' In *Singing Early Music: The Pronunciation of European Languages in the Late Middle Ages and Renaissance*, ed. Timothy J. McGee, pp 46–61 (Bloomington 1996).

Robert Grosseteste. *Templum Dei*. Ed. Joseph Goering and F.A.C. Mantello. Toronto Medieval Latin Texts 14 (Toronto 1984).

Robertson, D.W., Jr. 'A Note on the Classical Origin of "Circumstances" in the Medieval Confessional.' *Studies in Philology* 43.1 (1946) 6–14.

Rosemann, Philipp W. *The Story of a Great Medieval Book: Peter Lombard's* Sentences (Peterborough, ON 2007).

Russell, Josiah Cox. *Dictionary of Writers of Thirteenth-Century England*. Bulletin of the Institute of Historical Research, Special Supplement 3 (London 1936).

Saccenti, Ricardo. 'Questions et Sentences: L'enseignement entre la fin du XIIe et le début du XIIIe siècle.' In *Les débuts de l'enseignement universitaire à Paris (1200–1245 environ)*, ed. Jacques Verger and Olga Weijers, pp 275–293. Studia Artistarum 38 (Turnhout 2013).

Sanford, E.M. 'Giraldus Cambrensis' Debt to Petrus Cantor.' *Medievalia et Humanistica* 3 (1945) 16–32.

Schulte, Johann Friedrich, ed. *Decretistarum jurisprudentiae specimen: E libro Gottwicensi 88 (181) saeculo xii. manuscripto* (Giessen 1868).

Serlo of Savigny and Serlo of Wilton. *Seven Unpublished Works*. Ed. and trans. Lawrence C. Braceland. Cistercian Fathers 48 (Kalamazoo, MI 1987).

Servius. *In Vergilii carmina commentarii*. Ed. Georg Thilo and Hermann Hagen. Bibliotheca Teubneriana (Leipzig 1881–1902).

Sharpe, Richard. 'Reconstructing the Medieval Library of Bury St Edmunds Abbey: The Lost Catalogue of Henry of Kirkstead.' In *Bury St Edmunds: Medieval Art, Architecture, Archaeology, and Economy*, ed. Antonia Gransden, pp 204–218. Conference Transactions 20 (Leeds 1998).

Sharpe, Richard, James P. Carley, Rodney M. Thomson, and Andrew G. Watson, eds. *English Benedictine Libraries: The Shorter Catalogues*. Corpus of British Medieval Library Catalogues 4 (London 1996).

Simon of Tournai. *Disputationes*. Ed. Joseph Warichez. Spicilegium sacrum Lovaniense, Études et documents 12 (Leuven 1932).

——. 'Simon of Tournai's Commentary on the So-Called Athanasian Creed.' Ed. Nikolaus M. Häring. *Archives d'histoire doctrinale et littéraire du moyen âge* 43 (1976) 135–199.

Smalley, Beryl and George Lacombe. 'The Lombard's Commentary on Isaias and Other Fragments.' *The New Scholasticism* 5.2 (1931) 123–162.

Stotz, Peter. *Handbuch zur lateinischen Sprache des Mittelalters*. Handbuch der Altertumswissenschaft 2.5 (Munich 1996–2004).

Sulpicius Severus. *Vie de saint Martin*. Ed. Jacques Fontaine. Sources chrétiennes 133–135 (Paris 1967–1969).

Tanner, Thomas. *Bibliotheca Britannico-Hibernica, siue, De scriptoribus, qui in Anglia, Scotia, et Hibernia ad saeculi XVII initium floruerunt, commentarius*. Ed. David Wilkins (London 1748).

Thomas of Chobham. *Sermones*. Ed. Franco Morenzoni. CCCM 82a (Turnhout 1993).

——. *Summa de arte praedicandi*. Ed. Franco Morenzoni. CCCM 82 (Turnhout 1988).

——. *Summa de commendatione uirtutum et extirpatione uitiorum*. Ed. Franco Morenzoni. CCCM 82b (Turnhout 1997).

Thomson, Rodney M. 'The Library and Archives of Bury St. Edmunds Abbey' (PhD thesis, University of Sydney, 1974).

Valgimogli, Lorenzo. *Lo* Speculum Gregorii *di Adalberto di Metz*. Archivum Gregorianum 8 (Florence 2006).

van Liere, Frans. 'The Study of Canon Law and the Eclipse of the Lincoln Schools, 1175–1225.' *History of Universities* 18 (2003) 1–13.

West, J.R., ed. *St. Benet of Holme, 1020–1210*. The eleventh and twelfth century sections of Cott. Ms. Galba E. ii., the register of the abbey of St. Benet of Holme. Norfolk Record Society 2–3 (Fakenham, Norfolk 1932).

William of Conches. *Glosae super Platonem*. Ed. Édouard Jeauneau. CCCM 203 (Turnhout 2006).

William of Malmesbury. *Liber super explanationem Lamentationum Ieremiae prophetae*. Ed. Michael Winterbottom and Rodney M. Thomson. CCCM 244 (Turnhout 2011).

Winroth, Anders. *The Making of Gratian's* Decretum. Cambridge Studies in Medieval Life and Thought, 4th ser., 49 (Cambridge 2000).

Samvel Presbiter

Collecta ex diversis avditis in scola magistri Willelmi de Monte

Edited from
Oxford, Bodleian Library
MS Bodley 860

HEC COLLECTA SVNT EX DIVERSIS AVDITIS IN SCOLA MAGISTRI WILLELMI DE MONTE

1. In his primis ostenditur quod liberum arbitrium cooperatur gratie *94r*

Nulli cernentur oculis que subicientur
Ni lux exterior assit et interior.
Nulli cernentur celestia ni socientur
Bina: dei donum gratia, uelle bonum.

Duo necessaria sunt ad hoc ut aliquid uideatur usu corporeo: claritas exterior et uisus interior. **[3–4]**

interior: Lux interior, id est uisus interior. **[4]**

Ad hoc quod aliquis uideat spiritualia oportet quod duo concurrant: gratia dei et bona uoluntas. Vnde in psalmo dicitur: *Conserua me domine, quoniam speraui in te,* id est, Serua me mecum. Per hoc notatur quod liberum arbitrium cooperatur gratie. Et notandum quod quedam auctoritates attribuunt totum gratie dei, et hoc contra Peligianos qui dicunt liberum arbitrium sufficere absque gratia ad meritum uite eterne. Quedam auctoritates attribuunt totum libero arbitrio, et hoc contra pigros qui reputant gratia conferri bonum absque libero arbitrio et illorum conamine. Quedam auctoritates parciuntur, et attribuunt partem gratie, partem libero arbitrio. Vnde Paulus dicit: *Non ego sed gratia dei mecum. Dei enim adiutores sumus*. Sed licet **[5–6]**

1 3 *subicientur*: 'laid before' (*DMLBS* s.v. *subicere* 2)

7–32 *Duo…causa*: the discussion here is very similar to that in Peter Lombard, *Sententiae* 2.26–28 (including the references to Pelagianism and the idea of prevenient grace).

12 *Conserua…te*: Ps 15:1

12–14 *Serua…gratie*: this also appears in *Ex auditis super psalmos*, Ps 15:1 (fol. 21rb): *Conserua me domine*, id est, O pater simul serua me mecum. Per hoc quod dicitur, 'conser⟨ua⟩,' potest notari diuersitas personarum, et quod liberum arbitrium cooperatur gratie.

14–23 *quedam…principalitas*: this passage also appears in *Ex auditis super psalmos*, Ps 24:1 (fol. 37va–b).

20–21 *Non…mecum*: 1 Cor 15:10

21 *Dei…sumus*: 1 Cor 3:9

liberum arbitrium cooperetur gratie, tamen gratia preuenit, et in ea est principalitas. Vnde ait quidam:

Quicquid habes meriti, preuentrix gratia donat;
Nil deus in nobis preter sua dona coronat.

Et in oratione dicitur: 'Gratia tua domine nos preueniat et sequatur.' Gratia preuenit ut homo bonum uelit; sequitur ne frustra uelit. Gratia semper preuenit liberum arbitrium naturali ordine et causa licet non tempore. Infusio gratie causa est quare conuertatur homo ad deum. Sed quam cito infunditur gratia, et conuertitur homo ad deum! Et ita gratia non preuenit tempore, sed naturali ordine et causa.

2. Hic notantur sex, quorum obseruatio necessaria est sacerdoti

Absque parentela Salem rex atque sacerdos
Melchisedech Abrahe panem uinumque reuerso
Optulit occurrens; decimas tulit huic benedicens.
Sex istis uerbis notet esse tenenda sacerdos:
Sit—non carnalis affectu—spiritualis, *94v*
Occurrensque pie sit discretus modicusque
Curet sollicite se pacificare suosque;

24–25 *Quicquid…coronat*: cited by William de Montibus, *Tropi*, under 'Item gratia' (Goering, *William de Montibus*, 362); Walther, *Initia*, no. 15985

26–27 *Gratia…sequatur*: a paraphrase of what first appears in the Gregorian Sacramentary as the collect for the seventeenth Sunday after Pentecost (ed. Deshusses, no. 1177; sixteenth in later usage) and as a prayer for Vespers or Matins (no. 966)

2 3–13 This discussion refers to Hebr 7:1–10 and Gen 14:17–20. These verses also appear in William de Montibus, *Versarius*, under 'Melchisedech' (fol. 68r).

3–4 These verses are unrhymed.

3 *parentela*: 'lineage' (*DMLBS* s.v. *parentela* 3)

4 This verse is adapted from below, 37.6 (which includes the rhyme one expects).
Abrahe: consistently scanned *Ăbrăham* throughout the work

6 *Sex*: to be taken with *tenenda*
sacerdos: also the subject for the remaining verses

1.28 uelit *corr. in MS from* uelut **2.1** necessaria *subst. for* nescessaria *MS* **2.8–13** *Arabic numerals 1–6 add. to the left of these verses in MS by another hand*

Se regat atque suos, precibus se curet et ipsos;
Fiat communi iustus rex utilitati;
Conficiat limphe paulo cum pane meroque;
Spirituale serat, decimas oblataque sumat.

[3] *Absque parentela*: In hoc notatur spiritualitas. Dicit Paulus de eo: *Sine patre, sine matre, sine genealogia, nec inicium dierum neque finem uite habens, assimilatus filio dei, manet sacerdos in eternum.*
Salem: 'Salem' interpretatur pax. In hoc notatur officium sacerdotii, scilicet quod sacerdos debeat pacificare se et alios.
rex…sacerdos: In hoc quod dicitur, 'rex et sacerdos,' notatur ordinis dignitas quam habet sacerdos si per sapientiam se et alios regat.

[4] *Melchisedech*: 'Malchos' rex et 'Sadoc' iustus. Inde 'Melchisedech,' quasi rex iustus. Sic notatur publica utilitas quam debet sacerdos attendere sicut iustus rex attendit.
panem uinumque: In hoc quod dicitur, 'panem et uinum,' notatur ritus sacrificii quem debet sacerdos seruare conficiendo corpus Cristi cum pane et uino, paululo aque mixto cum uino.
reuerso: A cede quatuor regum.

[5] *Optulit occurrens*: In hoc quod dicitur, 'op⟨tulit⟩ oc⟨currens⟩,' notatur liberalitas. In hoc quod dicitur, 'op⟨tulit⟩ pa⟨nem⟩ et ui⟨num⟩,' notatur liberalitas moderata. In hoc quod dicitur, 'op⟨tulit⟩ Abrahe'—iusto uiro et suis reuersis a cede ·iiii· regum, qui inpugnauerunt ·v· reges, et fatigatis itinere et esurientibus—notatur liberalitas discreta. Sic per liberalitatem moderatam

12 *Conficiat*: understand *corpus Cristi* as the object (cf. lines 27–28). *limphe* = *lymphae*
15–17 *Sine…eternum*: Hebr 7:3
18 *Salem…pax*: *Glosa interl.* to Hebr 7:2; cf. Jerome, *Liber interpretationis hebraicorum nominum* 10 (CCSL 72:72, line 31).
19 *pacificare*: 'to keep in peace' or 'to protect' (*DMLBS* s.v. *pacificare* 6)
21 *ordinis dignitas*: 'the dignity of the office'
22 *alios regat*: cf. 1 Tim 5:17 and below, 4.20.
23–24 *Malchos…iustus*: cf. *Glosa interl.* to Hebr 7:2.
27 *conficiendo*: 'by consecrating' (*DMLBS* s.v. *conficere* 3)
29 *A…regum*: cf. Hebr 7:1.

2.10 curet: *another hand adds* uel mundet *above the line* **2.18** salem interpretatur pax: *appears after* alios regat (*line 22*) *in MS; I have transposed it to this location*

et discretam et spiritualitatem superius assignatam intelligitur conuersationis sanctitas, quam debet habere sacerdos. *decimas*: In hoc notatur uite regularitas quam debet habere sacerdos. Debet seminare spiritualia, et metere carnalia, scilicet uiuere de decimis et oblationibus sicut Leuite in ueteri testamento.

Scilicet conuersationis sanctitatem, officium sacerdotii, ordinis dignitatem, publicam utilitatem, ritum sacrificii, uite regularitatem. **[6]**

Id est habeat spiritualem et non carnalem affectum. **[7]**

Id est habeat liberalitatem discretam et moderatam, quam habens et spiritualitatem, habebit conuersationis sanctitatem. **[8]**

Sic seruabit officium sacerdotii. **[9]**

Sic seruabit ordinis dignitatem: regendo se et alios, et orando pro se et pro aliis. **[10]**

Id est attendat puplicam utilitatem sicut iustus rex debet attendere. **[11]**

Sic seruabit ritum sacrificii: paululum aque debet commisceri cum uino ut absorbeatur ab eo et consubstantietur ei. Sic mistice intelligitur quod fidelis populus consubstantiabitur Cristo. Per aquam accipitur fidelis populus; per uinum sanguis Cristi. **[12]**

Sic seruabit uite regularitatem. **[13]**

3. De spirituali oblatione, secundum oblationem sacrificii Abrahe

'Offerto trimam uaccam, capram quoque trimam.
Assit et his aries trimus, nec caonis ales
Nec turtur desit.' Abraham sic sacrificauit:

40–41 *uiuere... testamento*: cf. Num 18:24.
40 *decimis et oblationibus*: cf. below, 49.10.
53 *consubstantietur*: 'made of one substance' (*DMLBS* s.v. *consubstantiare*)

3 3–7 This section refers to Gen 15:9–11, and also appears in William de Montibus, *Versarius*, under 'Oblatio' (fol. 81v).
4 *caonis* = *chaonis* (cf. Ovid, *Ars amatoria* 2.150)

Hic tria diuisit, sed aues non dissociauit.
Hec dum sacra tulit muscas a carne fugauit.

uaccam: Per uaccam, que sub iugo est, accipitur obedientia, [3] que triplex debet esse, scilicet in obediendo legi naturali et legi scripte (scilicet legi mosayce) et ewangelio. Obedientia debet esse hilaris, cita, discreta, integra.
capram: Per capram, que offerebatur in ueteri testamento pro peccatis, accipitur penitentia, que debet esse triplex: per contritionem, per confessionem, per satisfactionem. Debet etiam esse triplex in deflendo preterita, demittendo presentia, cauendo futura. Confessio debet esse uoluntaria, munda, nuda, integra siue indiuisa.

aries: Per arietem, qui est dux gregis, accipitur intentio, que de- [4] bet esse triplex, quia fidelis debet intendere placere deo, mereri sibi, prodesse proximo.
caonis ales: Per columbam, que simplex est, accipitur simplicitas, quam debet homo offerre. Et sicut columba gregatim uolat et eligit meliora grana quando pascit se, et sicut super ripam fluminis uisa umbra accipit⟨r⟩is cauet sibi, sic fidelis consortia bonorum et suffragia querere debet et in sacra scriptura pociora eligere quibus pascat se, et uisis insidiis hostis per sacram scripturam sibi cauere.

7 *muscas*: also used in relation to the Gen 15:11 by Gerald of Wales, *Gemma Ecclesiastica* 2.33 (ed. Brewer, 327). The added gloss provides the Vulg. reading.

21–24 *columbam…accipitris*: the contrast between doves and hawks is found in a number of places in classical literature (e.g. Horace, *Carmina* 1.37.16–17; Ovid, *Metamorphoses* 5.605–606), and in this form seems to come ultimately from Rufinus's translation of Origen, *In Leuiticum homiliae* 3.8 (ed. Baehrens, 1:314, lines 12–16). For contemporary uses, see for instance William of Malmesbury, *Liber super explanationem Lamentationum Ieremiae prophetae* 1 (CCCM 244:95, lines 2505–2517) and Hugh de Fouilloy, *De columba et accipitre* (discussed in Carruthers, *The Book of Memory*, 303–309).

25 *suffragia*: 'prayers' (*DMLBS* s.v. *suffragium* 5)

3.7 muscas: *another hand adds* uel uolucres *above the line;* uel *originally omitted* (*this reading is integrated into the corresponding line in* Versarius) **3.11** hilaris *corr. in MS from* ylaris *by another hand* **3.24** umbra *subst. for* iutibra *MS* **3.25** suffragia *subst. for* sustragia *MS*

turtur: Per turturem, que casta auis est, accipitur castitas, quam [5]
debet offere fidelis. Et sicut turtur habet gemitum pro cantu, sic fidelis debet habere gemitum pro peccatis suis, pro peccatis alienis, pro dilatione glorie, pro presentia miserie, dicendo cum propheta: *Heu mihi, quia incolatus meus,* etc.
Abraham: Abraham optulit hec ·v· in sacrificium—scilicet uaccam, capram, arietem, columbam, turturem—secundum precepta domini.

hic tria diuisit: Per hoc intelligitur quod opera possunt diuidi [6]
secundum diuersitatem temporum, prout rerum uarietas exigit. Excerciis diuersorum operum diuersa competunt tempora, et aliquando requiescendum est operibus intermissis ad horam.
aues non dissociauit: Sed castitas et simplicitas semper habende sunt coniuncte.

Musce sibi inuicem succedentes perdunt suauitatem odoris, id [7]
est uane cogitationes mentem distrahentes perdunt suauitatem orationis. Has debet fidelis fugare dum deo aliquid offert.

4. Hic monetur ut qui uult fieri rector populi prius precellat in sapientia et bonis mo⟨ri⟩bus

Hic qui uult Abraham fieri, fiat prius Abram. *95r*
Sic in Bersabee plantare potest nemus ille,

32 *Heu…meus*: Ps 119:5

38 *Excerciis = exercitiis*

38–39 *Excerciis…horam*: 'different actions are appropriate at different times, and sometimes one should stop work and rest for a short time.'

39 *ad horam*: 'for a short time,' 'temporarily' (*DMLBS* s.v. *1 hora* 6b)

42 *Musce…odoris*: Eccl 10:1 (*sibi inuicem succedentes* for Vulg. *morientes*)

43–44 *uane…offert*: cf. Gregory the Great, *Moralia in Iob* 16.42.53 (CCSL 143a:829, lines 21–29). This is vividly illustrated in the Lambeth Apocalypse; facsimiles in Morgan, *The Lambeth Apocalypse,* fol. 53r (commentary, 257–259) and Morgan, *Early Gothic Manuscripts,* pt. 2, ill. 141.

4 3–7 These verses also appear in William de Montibus, *Versarius*, under 'Nemus Abrahe' (fol. 77v).

4.1 populi *subst. for* popopuli *MS*

In quo latrones, uermesque, ferasque feroces,
Atque feras mites, et robora celsa, uolucres
Attendat. Saltus inter uepres sit amenus.

[3] 'Abba,' pater; 'ham,' multarum. Inde 'Abraham,' quasi *pater multarum gentium.* 'Abba,' pater; 'rama,' excelsum. Inde 'Abram,' quasi pater excelsus.
Abraham: Id est *pater multarum gentium.*
Abram: Id est pater excelsus in sapientia et bonis moribus.

[4] Bersabee fuit puteus siue fons iuxta quem *Abraham plantauit nemus.* Et interpretatur 'septimus puteus,' iuxta quem—id est iuxta septiformem gratiam spiritus, uel iuxta sacram scripturam, que est quasi puteus propter profundas sententias—pater excelsus in sapientia et bonis moribus potest plantare nemus: scilicet habendo septiformem gratiam spiritus et habendo cognitionem sacre scripture plantare potest nemus, id est multos conuocare, eos docendo uel eos regendo.

[5] *latrones*: Scilicet ypocritas, qui latent in pelle ouina.
uermesque: Serpentes uenenosos, scilicet inuidos.
ferasque feroces: Vrsos, leones; scilicet iracundos, elatos.

[6] *feras mites*: Scilicet illos qui uoluntarie et cum mansuetudine feruntur ad diuersa officia, et sunt fere ruminantes (scilicet psallentes orando et repetentes que repetenda sunt) et habent ungulam fissam (scilicet discretionem inter sensum littere superficialem et sensum spiritualem).
robora: Scilicet fortes et prouectos in uirtutibus.
uolucres: Scilicet illos qui plurimum uacant contemplationi et uolant secus firmamentum sicut aues. Et possunt iam dicere:

7 *Saltus*: i.e. part of the *nemus* (*DMLBS* s.v. *3 saltus* 2)
8–11 *Abba…gentium*: Gen 17:5 and its *Glosa interl.*
13–14 *Bersabee…nemus*: Gen 21:33
14 *septimus puteus*: *Glosa interl.* to Gen 21:31
15–16 *sacram…puteus*: *Glosa marg.* to Gen 21:31
20 *eos regendo*: cf. above, 2.22.
25–27 *ruminantes…fissam*: cf. Deut 14:6.

4.6 celsa *subst.* (*with Versarius: Cambridge, Corpus Christi College, MS 186, fol. 77v*) *for* cessa *MS* **4.24** cum *om. MS before corr.*

Nostra conuersatio in celis est.

attendat: Vt illos corrigat, alios in perseuerantia conseruet. [7]
saltus…amenus: Inter uarios rigores per amenam dispensationem debet fieri recreatio.

5. Hic notantur duo que necessaria sunt ad delendum et cauendum peccata

Inter Sur, Cades, Abraham posuit sibi sedes.
  Crimen in his delet uir bonus atque cauet.
Iudicii fons est Cades; angustia Sur est.
  Hos inter sapias, et bene peniteas.

'Sur' interpretatur angustia, 'Cades' fons iudicii. [3]

Scilicet in sedibus inter angustiam (per quam accipitur peniten- [4–5]
tia) et fontem iudicii (scilicet discretionis, per quam accipitur sapientia, que cauet peccatum) penitentia delet.

Scilicet inter fontem iudicii, in quo sapit homo, et angustiam, [6]
in qua penitet.
sapias: Cauendo peccata.
peniteas: Delendo peccata.

6. Hic monetur in domino gaudere

Cum strue lignorum ponas Ysaac super altum.
  Non perimentur ibi gaudia fixa tibi.

32 *Nostra…est*: Phil 3:20

5 3–6 This section refers to Gen 20:1. These verses also appear in William de Montibus, *Versarius*, under 'Mansio Abrae' (fol. 68r).

7 *Sur…iudicii*: *Glosa interl.* to Gen 20:1

6 2–3 This section refers to Gen 22:2. These verses also appear in William de Montibus, *Versarius*, under 'Immolatio Isaach' (fol. 77v).

5.3 posuit: *another hand adds* uel legit *above the line* **5.7** iudicii *subst. for* iudicicii *MS*

[2] 'Ysaac' interpretatur risus. Sicut Abraham fecit struem lignorum et optulit Ysaac in monte cum apparatione mactationis, sic fidelis apparatus ad mactationem offerre debet Ysaac in monte, scilicet gaudere in domino semper, sicut dicit apostolus: *Gaudete in domino semper.* Et debet facere struem lignorum, scilicet imitatione digna sumpta a sanctis patribus habere in memoria imitando ea, sicut iusticiam Abel, pacientiam Iob, fidem Abrahe, mansuetudinem Moysi, laborem Noe siue longanimitatem.

[3] Scilicet gaudia in excelso, id est in deo reposita, non adnihilabuntur (sicut nec Ysaac peremptus est) sed illa fient ampliora.

7. De iuramento

Iuramenta deo reddas; tribus hec reuocato. *95v*
Sed tibi precipue licet hec propter tria ferre:
Vero, iusticia, tu iuditio quoque iura.
Si tres hii desunt, comites periuria fiunt.

[1] Per hoc intelligitur quod tantum per deum iurandum est et quod soluendum est. Iuramentum non est iurandum per creaturas, ita quod aliquid numinis credatur inesse creaturis, uel ut ueneratio debita creatori exhibeatur eis. Sed licet quandoque iurare per creaturam subintellecto auctore creature et exibita ei ueneratione sub tali forma iurandi. Dicitur quod Ioseph iurando *per salutem Pharaonis* auctorem salutis Pharaonis in eo ueneratus est. Soluendum est iuramentum nisi reuocet auctoritas

4 *Ysaac…risus*: cf. Gen 21:6.
8 *Gaudete in domino semper*: Phil 4:4
9–10 *imitatione…ea*: 'store up things worthy of imitation taken from the holy fathers in memory by following them.'
10–12 *iusticiam…longanimitatem*: cf. Gregory the Great, *Moralia in Iob,* Praef.6.7.

7 10 *exibita = exhibita*
11–13 *Ioseph…est[1]*: cf. Peter Lombard, *Sententiae* 3.39.5.2; Gratian, C.22 q.1 d.p. c.16; below, 19.19–21.
12 *per salutem Pharaonis*: Gen 42:15–16

7.8 inesse *subst. for* ineesse *MS* **7.11** tali *corr. in MS from* tati

ecclesie, uel impediat necessitas uel iniquitas (scilicet mortale peccatum).

Iuramenta maxime habent fieri propter testimonia ferenda, [2]
propter pacta confirmanda, propter scandala tollenda (scilicet ut aliquis expers criminis sibi impositi purget se a tali crimine).

uero: Vt conscientia dictet esse uerum quod iuratur. [4]
iusticia: Vt de re licita fiat iuramentum.
iuditio: Scilicet in discretione, quia non debet quis precipitanter et sponte iurare, sed quadam exactione et necessitate conpulsus.

tres: Scilicet ueritas, iusticia, iuditium. [5]
periuria: Periurium quandoque dicitur perperam iuratum, quandoque falso iuramento firmatum, quandoque dicitur mutatio iuramenti.

8. De humilitate

Te sub maiori, te sub pare siue minori,
Te bene das humilem si cadis in faciem.
Si tu sis humilis uere, tu te bene noscis,
Vilescisque tibi cognitione tui.
Inquiras quid habes, a quo, quam labile serues:
Sic conseruaris in tribus his humilis.
Corde geras humilem te paruum cordeque mitem.
Cristus sic mitem se docet ac humilem.

Vnus est gradus humilitatis humiliare se maiori; alius gradus [2]
est humiliare se pari; tercius et summus gradus est humiliare se minori. Hanc humilitatem habuit Cristus lauando pedes discipulorum.

Qui cadit in faciem uidet quo cadet. Abraham *cecidit in faciem* [3]
domino loquente cum eo: sic notatur quod discreta debet esse

14 *iniquitas*: cf. *illicitudo* below, 55.59.

8 14 *Qui…cadet*: cf. Heiric of Auxerre, *Homiliae per circulum anni* 1.65 (CCCM 116a:645, lines 102–103)
14–15 *Abraham…eo*: Gen 17:3, 17:17

8.3 cadis *corr. in MS from* cades **8.5** cognitione *corr. in MS from* cognatione **8.9** ac *corr. in MS from* hac **8.10** se *om. MS before corr.; add. above the line*

humilitas. Si est discreta (in quocumque gradu sit), est humilitas gratie, meritoria uite. Quedam humilitas est nature, que est in paruulis. Vnde dicitur: *Qui se humiliat ut paruulus,* etc. Est humiliatio culpe. Vnde illud: *Est qui nequiter humiliat se et inceriora eius plena sunt dolo.* Est humiliatio pene. Vnde illud: *Qui se exaltat humiliabitur,* id est deicietur.

Humilitas est uirtus qua homo uerissima sui cognitione sibi ipsi [4–5]
uilescit.

quid: Sic inuenis te imperfectum in naturalibus bonis et gratui- [6]
tis.
a quo: Sic inuenis te nihil habere pro⟨pri⟩um.
quam: Sic inuenis quod timeas ruinam bonorum que habes.

Qui attente considerat se esse inperfectum, nihil habere pro- [7]
prium, defacili posse amittere bona que habet, conseruare poterit humilitatem.

Humilitas et mansuetudo in corde debent esse site. [8]

Cristus ait: *Discite a me, quia mitis sum et humilis corde.* [9]

9. De mansuetudine

Si tu mitis eris, scripturis erudieris.
Applaudent homines: regna superna petes. *96r*

Est mansuetudo nature. Vnde illud: 'Homo est animal mansue- [2]
tum natura.' Est man⟨suetudo⟩ culpe, qua ostendit se care⟨re⟩

17 *meritoria*: 'deserving (of),' 'worthy (of)' (*DMLBS* s.v. *meritorius* 1)
18 *Qui…paruulus*: a conflation of Lc 14:11 or 18:14 with Mt 18:4
19–20 *Est…dolo*: Eccli 19:23
inceriora = *interiora*
21 *Qui…humiliabitur*: Lc 14:11, 18:14
29 *de facili*: 'easily'
32 *Discite…corde*: Mt 11:29

9 4–5 *Homo…natura*: adapted from Boethius's translation of Aristotle, *Topica* 5.8, 138a10 (ed. Minio-Paluello, 5.1:110, lines 20–22), which was revived in the twelfth century.

8.26 sic…proprium *corr. in MS over eras.* **8.28–29** proprium *corr. in MS from* perprium **8.32** corde *corr. in MS from* cordi

quidam conuolans ad claustrum, dicens patri: Mitius inuenies quam me genus omne ferarum, nec reuocare potes me pro fluuio lacrimarum. Est man⟨suetudo⟩ gratie, de qua dicitur: *Beati mites, quoniam ipsi hereditabunt terram,* scilicet ter⟨ram⟩ uiuentium. Hec man⟨suetudo⟩ tria comparat: gratiam apud homines; intelligentiam in sacra scriptura (unde illud: *Diriget mansuetos in iudicio; docebit mites uias suas*); comparat et gloriam in futuro (unde illud: *Exaltabit mansuetos in salutem*).

'Mansuetus' dicitur quasi 'manu assuetus,' scilicet socialis et [3]
tractabilis tali uiro. 'Applaudent homines' manifeste exterius et interius affectu, et tandem exaltabitur in eternam salutem.

10. De lacrimis

Gratia, si lacrimis assit, solamen habebis.
  Non hoc sed lacrimis dat mala culpa suis.

Sunt lacrime gratie, scilicet penitentiales. Vnde dicitur in psal- [2]
mo penitentiali: *Lauabo per singulas noctes lectum meum; lacrimis meis stratum meum rigabo.* Has lacrimas habuit Petrus, qui negato Cristo *fleuit amare*; et Maria Magda⟨lena⟩, que rigauit lacrimis pedes domini. Aliquis habet has lacri⟨mas⟩

6–7 *Mitius…ferarum*: cf. Ovid, *Heroides* 10.1: 'Mitius inveni quam te genus omne ferarum.'
9 *Beati…terram*[1]: Mt 5:4 (*hereditabunt* for Vulg. *possedebunt*, perhaps via Ps 36:11, esp. in the translation from the Hebrew)
11–12 *Diriget…suas*: Ps 24:9
13 *Exaltabit…salutem*: Ps 149:4

10 3 *mala culpa*: construe, *Culpa lacrimis suis non hoc sed mala dat.*
4–5 *psalmo penitentiali*: Pss. 6, 31, 37, 50, 101, 129, and 142 were designated as 'penitential,' originally in Cassiodorus's commentary (as repeated in Peter Lombard, *Commentarium in Psalmos,* Ps. 50.intro (PL 191:484a).
5–6 *Lauabo…rigabo*: Ps 6:7
7 *fleuit amare*: Mt 26:75
8 *rigauit…domini*: cf. Lc 7:38.

10.2 lacrimis *corr. in MS from* lacrim**

pro peccatis alienis. Vnde Paulus: *Quis infirmatur et ego non infirmor?* Sunt etiam lacrime gratie que fiunt pro presentia miserie (unde: *Super flumina Babilonis illic*, etc.), et que fiunt pro dila⟨tione⟩ glorie (unde illud: *Fuerunt mihi lacrime mee panis*, etc.). *Heu mihi, quia incolatus meus prolongatus est*, etc. Hoc etiam potest legi pro presentia miserie et pro dila⟨tione⟩ glorie. Dicitur: *Beati qui lugent, quoniam ipsi consolabuntur.* Alibi dicitur: *Absterget deus omnem lacrimam ab oculis sanctorum.*

Sunt quedam lacrime culpe, scilicet lacrime cupiditatis (de [3]
quibus dicitur: ‘Ploratur lacrimis amissa pecunia ueris’) et lacrime desperationis (unde Paulus ait: *Nolo uos ignorare de dormientibus, ut non contristemini, sicut et ceteri qui spem non habent*). He lacrime, scilicet cupiditatis et desperationis, sunt detestabiles. Sunt quedamlacrime nature (scilicet la⟨crime⟩ naturales) et humane affectionis, humane pietatis et compassionis. Huiusmodi lacrimas habuit Cristus quando fleuit Lazarum.

11. De esurie spirituali

Est grauis illa fames doctrine pane carentes.
   Que facit, hanc caueas, hac male ne pereas.
Praua fames absit; deus esuriem saciabit,
   Si desiderium constat habere pium.
Vrbem circueat hic qui fore doctor hanelat;

9–10 *Quis... infirmor*: 2 Cor 11:29
11 *Super... illic*: Ps 136:1
12–13 *Fuerunt... panis*: Ps 41:4
13 *Heu... est*: Ps 119:5
15–16 *Beati... consolabuntur*: Mt 5:5
16–17 *Absterget... sanctorum*: Apoc 21:4 (*sanctorum* for Vulg. *eorum*)
19 *Ploratur... ueris*: Juvenal, 13.134
20–22 *Nolo... habent*: 1 Thess 4:13
25 *Cristus... Lazarum*: Io 11:35; cf below, 20.7, 30.16–17.

11 6 *hanelat = anhelat*

10.11 unde: ** *add. MS before corr.* **10.20** desperationis *corr. in MS from* disperationis **10.23** quedam *corr. in MS from* quidam

Vt doctor fiat, ut canis esuriat.
Sanguisuge natas numquam plene saciatas,
Vis tua luxuriam trudat, auariciam.

Est quedam fames defectus et penurie, de qua dominus ait: **[2–3]** *Mittam eis famem: non famem panis, nec sitim aque, sed audiendi uerbum dei*. Hec multum metuenda est. Est quedam esuries et sitis nature: hanc esuriem habuit etiam Cristus. Vnde dicitur: *Cum ieiunasset ·xl· diebus et ·xl· noctibus postea esuriit*. Hanc esuriem habet in menbris. Vnde dicitur: *Esuriui et dedistis mihi panem*. Sitim etiam habens, dixit Samaritane: *Da mihi bibere*.

Est fames siue sitis praui desiderii sicut luxuria siue philargiria. **[4–5]** Est fames siue sitis boni desiderii. Vnde dicitur: *Beati qui esuriunt et sitiunt iusticiam, quoniam ipsi saturabuntur*. Et alibi dicitur: *Esurientes impleuit bonis*. Et alibi dicitur:

Quo fruuntur nec fastidiunt,
Sed eo amplius frui sitiunt.

Id est qui affectat alios docere non sit piger sed strenuus cir- **[6]** cumeundo diuersa loca ut Cristus, qui *circuibat totam Galileam* predicando.

Predicator specialiter debet habere rapidam famem ut canis, ut **[7]** multos bonis moribus informet per doctrinam suam. In psalmo

8–9 *Sanguisuge…auariciam*: construe, *Vis tua trudat sanguisuge natas, numquam plene saciatas: luxuriam, auariciam.*

11–12 *Mittam…dei*: Am 8:11 (*mittam famem in terram* in Vulg.)

14–15 *Cum…esuriit*: Mt 4:2

15–16 *Esuriui…panem*: Mt 25:35 (*panem* for Vulg. *manducare*, perhaps via Gen 28:20)

16–17 *Da…bibere*: Io 4:7

19–20 *Beati…saturabuntur*: Mt 5:6

21 *Esurientes impleuit bonis*: Lc 1:53

22–23 *Quo…sitiunt*: cf. Adam of St Victor, *Superne matris gaudia* 35–36 (ed. Grosfillier, 461), a sequence hymn for All Saints' Day; cited in its original form in Peter the Chanter, *Verbum adbreuiatum*, textus conflatus 2.6 (CCCM 196:637, lines 77–78); textus prior 87 (CCCM 196a:525, lines 15–16); textus alter 73 (CCCM 196b:390, lines 83–84).

25 *circuibat totam Galileam*: Mt 4:23 (cf. below, 24.6)

27 *rapidam* = *rabidam*

dicitur: *Famem patientur ut canes et circuibunt ciuitatem.*

Dicit Salomon quod luxuria et philargiria *sunt due filie san-* [8–9]
guisuge, scilicet diaboli, qui dicit semper: *Affer, affer*. Insacia-
bilis est uorago libidinis. De auaricia dicitur:

Crescit amor nummi quantum ipsa pecunia crescit.

12. De misericordia

Tu dimitteris, tu premia digna sequeris, *96v*
Si dimissor eris, si benefactor eris.
Det uir ut accipiat; sua comodet ut sibi fiat
Iudex propicius. Retribuendo pius,
Vt dimittatur, dimittat; compaciatur,
Electique dei compatientur ei.
Discernas dando quid, cui, cur, quomodo, quando,
Quantum donabis: sic tua dona dabis.

Quatuor comitantur misericordiam: dare (unde illud: *Date et* [2]
dabitur uobis), dimittere (unde illud: *Dimittite et dimittetur*
uobis), comodare (unde illud: *Volenti mutuari ne auertaris*),
conpati (unde illud: *Flere cum flentibus, gaudere cum gauden-*
tibus). Conpassio et congratulatio sunt duo ubera sponse.

29 *Famem…ciuitatem*: Ps 58:7
30–33 *Dicit…crescit*[2]: cf. Peter the Chanter, *Verbum adbreuiatum*, textus conflatus 1.15 (CCCM 196:118, lines 67–76); textus prior 16 (CCCM 196a:120, lines 39–49); textus alter 73 (CCCM 196b:390, lines 90–95)
30–31 *sunt…affer*: Prov 30:15
33 *Crescit*[1]*…crescit*[2]: Juvenal, 14.139

12 8–9 *quid…Quantum*: Goering, *William de Montibus*, 395 identifies some sixty uses of these words (in what he calls 'circumstantial' poems) in William de Montibus, *Versarius*.
10–11 *Date et dabitur uobis*: Lc 6:38
11–12 *Dimittite et dimittetur uobis*: Lc 6:37
12 *Volenti…auertaris*: Mt 5:42
13–14 *Flere…gaudentibus*: Rom 12:15
14 *Conpassio…sponse*: cf. Bernard of Clairvaux, *Sermones super Cantica Canticorum* 10.1 (ed. Leclercq, Talbot, and Rochais,

11.29 ciuitatem *corr. in MS from* circuitatem **12.7** compatientur *corr. in MS from* compati*ntur

Si misericors fueris in remissione iniuriarum et collatione beneficiorum, misericordiam consequeris. **[3]**

Det: Det beneficia ut accipiat centupla. **[4]**
comodet: Comodet pauperibus ut deus pro eis retribuat in die iudicii. Dicit pauper: *Dominus retribuet pro me.*

In psalmo dicitur: *Iocundus homo qui miseretur et comodat; disponet sermones suos in iuditio.* Alibi dicitur: *Iustus tota die miseretur et comodat.* **[5]**

ut dimittatur: Debet quilibet dimittere alii rancorem et odium et iniurias siue iniurietur ei in afflictione corporis, siue in contumeliis, siue in dampno rei familiaris. Etsi sit perfectus, debet etiam dimittere signa rancoris et odii, et dicere ei: Aue. **[6]**
compaciatur: Miseriis proximorum, et habebit sanctos intercessores pro eo apud deum.

E contra erit de his qui non fecerunt misericordiam, quia dicitur: *Iudicium sine misericordia ei qui non fecerit misericordiam.* **[7]**

quid: Elemosinam. *Date elemosinam et omnia munda sunt uobis.* **[8]**
cui: Pauperibus. *Dispersit* (non congregauit), *dedit* (non uendidit), *pauperibus* (non diuitibus), quia habenti dare nihil aliud

---

1:49, lines 1–3), which relates this to the quotation from Romans; Bernard of Clairvaux, *Sententiae* 1.9, 1.31, 2.168 (ed. Leclercq and Rochais, 6.2:9, line 14; 18, line 3; 55, lines 21–22).

17 *accipiat centupla*: cf. Mt 19:29.

19 *Dominus…me*: Ps 137:8

20–21 *Iocundus…iuditio*: Ps 111:5

21–22 *Iustus…comodat*: Ps 36:26 (Vulg. omits *iustus*, but this is found in many commentaries.)

24–25 *siue*[1]*…familiaris*: cf. below, 15.30–31, and Peter the Chanter, *Verbum adbreuiatum*, textus conflatus 2.8 (CCCM 196:644, lines 3–7); textus alter 74 (CCCM 196b:394, lines 93–97).

30 *Iudicium…misericordiam*: Iac 2:13

31–32 *Date…uobis*: Lc 11:41

33–34 *Dispersit…pauperibus*: Ps 111:9

34–35 *habenti…perdere*: Gratian, C.1 q.2 c.7; cf. Peter the Chanter, *Verbum adbreuiatum*, textus conflatus 1.16, 1.45 (CCCM 196:138,

12.16 consequeris *subst. for* consequeretis, *corr. in MS from* consequerestis **12.23** debet quilibet *corr. in MS from* deb** *u*

est quam perdere. *Esurientes impleuit bonis.*
cur: Vt deus retribuat. *Date et dabitur uobis: mensuram bonam et confectam et cogitatam et supereffluentem dabit in sinum uestrum,* scilicet Cristus dabit pro pauperibus.
quomodo: Hilariter. *Hilarem datorem diligit deus.*
quando: Instanter. *Omne quod potest manus tua instanter operare.* Nescis quid pariat crastina dies.

quantum: Quod superest. *Omne quod superest, date elemosinam.* [9] Omne quod est ultra necessaria dandum est. Dicit Paulus: *Non ut aliis sit remissio, uobis autem tribulatio.* Dicit Ieronimus: 'Aliena rapere conuincitur, qui ultra necessaria retinere conprobatur.' Res pauperum sunt que supersunt necessariis et dande sunt pauperibus.

13. De mundicia

Illum conspiciet, si mundum cor tibi fiet,
Quem nisi mundus eris cernere non poteris.

Mundicia cordis prouehit hominem ad intellectum diuinitatis. [2]

---

lines 239–240; 299, lines 7–11).

35 *Esurientes impleuit bonis*: Lc 1:53

36–38 *Date...uestrum*: Lc 6:38

37 *confectam et cogitatam*: perhaps an error for Vulg. *confertam et coagitatam*, but both variants are attested elsewhere.

39 *Hilarem...deus*: 2 Cor 9:7

40–41 *Omne...operare*: Eccl 9:10

41 *Nescis...dies*: a paraphrase of Prov 27:1 similar to Peter the Chanter, *Verbum adbreuiatum*, textus conflatus 2.56 (CCCM 196:826, line 198); textus alter 102 (CCCM 196b:506, line 143)

42–43 *Omne...elemosinam*: Lc 11:41; cf. Gratian, C.16 q.1 c.47

44 *Non...tribulatio*: 2 Cor 8:13

45–46 *Aliena...conprobatur*: Gratian, D.42 d.a. c.1; also quoted by Peter the Chanter, *Verbum adbreuiatum*, textus conflatus 1.13 (CCCM 196:111–112, lines 268–269); textus prior 14 (CCCM 196a:114, lines 4–5); textus alter 13 (CCCM 196b:75, lines 218–219)

13 4 *Mundicia...diuinitatis*: cf. Mt 5:8

12.37 sinum *subst. for* sitium *MS* **12.42** quod superest[1] *om. MS before corr.* **12.47** pauperibus: *approximately eight following letters eras. in MS*

Dicitur de patre: [3]
Mundi cordis quem soli cernere possunt oculi.

14. De pace

Pax solide mentis, non temporis, est bona cunctis.
Hac poteris dici filius esse dei.
Pax quibus est mentis, dabitur pax summa perhennis.
Tu renuas mundi triplice pace frui. *97r*

Triplex est pax dei: pax temporis, pax pectoris, pax eternitatis. [2–3] Pax temporis indifferens est. Quibusdam est bona sicut infirmis in ecclesia qui facile scandalizarentur in persecutione. Et ideo ecclesia orat pro hac pace. Quibusdam est mala, his scilicet qui resoluuntur in pace. De Dauid dicitur: 'Vicit tranquillitas pacis quem bella non uicerant.' De pace pectoris dicitur: *Beati pacifici, quoniam filii dei uocabuntur.* Magna est dignitas huius uirtutis, cum faciat dici filium dei.

Dicit Cristus discipulis: *Pacem relinquo uobis,* scilicet pacem [3]

6 *Mundi... oculi*: from the sequence hymn for Pentecost, *Sancti spiritus assit nobis gratia*, verse 10, first recorded in Notker Balbulus, *Liber ymnorum* (ed. von den Steinen, 56)

14 2 *solide*: 'resolute' (*DMLBS* s.v. *solidus* 5)

4 *perhennis = perennis*

6 *pax*[2]*... eternitatis*: these categories are similarly defined in Peter the Chanter, *Verbum adbreuiatum*, textus conflatus 2.21 (CCCM 196:674, lines 17–21), 2.23 (681, lines 31–33); textus prior 100 (CCCM 196a:558–559, lines 8–9); textus alter 79 (CCCM 196b:412, lines 12–16).

10–11 *Vicit... uicerant*: this occurs with slightly different wording in Peter Lombard, *Commentarium in Psalmos*, Ps. 50.intro (PL 191:483d) and in the *Glosa interl.* to Ps 50:2; it is also found in Gerald of Wales, *Gemma ecclesiastica* 2.14 (ed. Brewer, 263); also found in *Ex auditis super psalmos*, Ps 4:9 (fol. 11rb).

11–12 *Beati... uocabuntur*: Mt 5:9

14 *Pacem... uobis*: Io 14:27

14.7 quibusdam *corr. in MS from* quibus **14.11** quem *corr. in MS from* que

pectoris, *pacem meam do uobis,* scilicet pacem eternitatis. Dicit 'do' utens presenti propter certitudinem.

Triplex est pax mundi. Pax proditorum. Vnde de Iuda dicitur: [5]
Homo pacis mee in quo speraui magnificauit super me supplantationem. Pax adulatorum. Vnde dicitur: *Pacem locuntur cum proximo suo, mala autem in cordibus eorum.* Et a propheta dicitur Sedechie: *Pacifici tui seduxerunt te,* scilicet, Adulatores tui seduxerunt te. Est et pax pigrorum. Vnde dicitur: *Zelaui super iniquos, pacem peccatorum uidens.* Et dicit diues: *Anima, habes multa bona. Requiesce.* Quasi diceret: A modo poteris pacem habere.

15. De pacientia

Quandoque nature, numquam pacientia culpe,
Sed semper prodest gratia cui comes est.
Consuetudine, spe, nature strenuitate
Hec uiget. Hec contra sit bene firma tria.

Est pacientia nature. Homo est animal patientissimum natu- [2–3]
ra. Est pacientia culpe, scilicet stolida pa⟨cientia⟩ et asinina, quando aliquis est patiens ultra debitum finem. Est pacientia gratie. Vnde dicitur: *Beati qui persecutionem patiuntur propter iusticiam, quoniam ipsorum est regnum celorum.*

16 *certitudinem*: 'certain knowledge' (*DMLBS* s.v. *certitudo*)
18–19 *Homo… supplantationem*: Ps 40:10
19–20 *Pacem… eorum*: Ps 27:3
locuntur = loquuntur
21 *Pacifici tui seduxerunt te*: Ier 38:22
22–23 *Zelaui… uidens*: Ps 72:3
23–24 *Anima… Requiesce*: Lc 12:19

15 6–7 *Homo… natura*: also cited in Peter the Chanter, *Verbum adbreuiatum*, textus conflatus 2.24 (CCCM 196:697, lines 373–374); textus alter 80 (CCCM 196b:425, lines 225–226).
9–10 *Beati… celorum*: Mt 5:10

14.21 seduxerunt *corr. in MS from* seducerunt **14.22** pigrorum *subst. for* pig*orum *MS, with letter eras. but not replaced*

Hec pars: 'Beati qui perse⟨cutionem⟩,' etc., octauo posita in ewangelio cum quolibet ·vii· premissorum. Intelligitur repetenda hoc modo: *Beati pauperes*, etc. si 'perse⟨cutionem⟩ patiuntur propter iusticiam'; *Beati mites*, si 'perse⟨cutionem⟩ pa⟨tiuntur⟩ propter iusticiam'; et ita de aliis.

consuetudine: 'Quod male fers, assuesse: feres.' [4]
spe:

Merces spectatur;
pene labor alleuiatur.

nature strenuitate: Aliquis habens strenuitatem nature ad martyrium sustinendum cicius animaretur aliquo contemplatiuo carenti tali strenuitate, licet esset melior eo et firmior in caritate.

Patientia habenda est contra flagella dei, ne faciant murmurare; contra temptamenta diaboli, ne faciant succumbere; contra hominem, 'ut non reddatur malum pro malo.' Contra odium hominis exhibenda est dilectio, secundum illud: *Diligite inimicos uestros*. Contra contumelias exhibenda est taciturnitas secundum illud: *Factus sum sicut homo non audiens et non habens in ore suo redargutiones*. Exhibenda est etiam pacientia contra hominem, si iniuriatus fuero in afflictione corporis, uel dampno rei familiaris. [5]

13 *Beati pauperes*: Mt 5:3

14 *Beati mites*: Mt 5:4

16 *Quod…feres*: Ovid, *Ars* 2.647; also quoted by Peter the Chanter, *Verbum adbreuiatum*, textus conflatus 2.24 (CCCM 196:697, line 376); textus prior 103 (CCCM 196a:578, line 220)

18–19 *Merces…alleuiatur*: the source for this is unclear; it is later found in a sermon of Luca da Bitonto for the feast of St Stephan (ed. Lombardo, 'Ecclesia huius temporis,' appendix 1, p. 28).

25 *ut…malo*: cf. Rom 12:17; the phrasing is from Augustine, *Contra Adimantum* 17 (CSEL 25.1:171, line 1), similarly writing 'de inimici dilectione.'

26–27 *Diligite inimicos uestros*: Mt 5:44; Lc 6:27, 6:35

28–29 *Factus…redargutiones*: Ps 37:15

30–31 *si…familiaris*: cf. above, 12.24–25.

15.11 posita *corr. in MS over eras. by another hand* **15.21** animaretur *subst. for* acumaretur *MS* **15.23** patientia *corr. in MS from* pacientiam **15.25** non *om. MS before corr.; add. in marg. by another hand* **15.28** illud *corr. in MS from* idem *by another hand*

16. Hic habetur instructio sumpta ex hoc quod Cristus in die sabbati surrexit legere, et in his monemur aptari his que legimus in sacra scriptura ibi in quibus possumus

Cristus surrexit; sibi tradita scripta reuoluit,
Legit, complicuit, famulo dedit, atque resedit.
Hec bene uerba nota: ·vii· sunt elicienda.
Significatiue non materialiter ipse
Verba reperta libri legit. Sic spirituali
Mente nitere stude. Possis uelut ipse referre:
Significatiue, distincte sic et aperte
'Spiritus' et reliqua que tradita sunt Ysaia. *97v*

Cristus in *die sabbati* inter seniores *surrexit legere*, in quo [5]
notatur quod paratum se exhibuit ad legendum. *Et traditus est ei liber* a ministro, in quo notatur quod non intrusit se.

Debemus surgere, bene operando; accipere librum, audiendo [7]
et discendo; reuoluere librum, memorando; legere, predicando; complicare, nos cum aliis reseruando; dare librum ministro, doctori uicem rependendo; residere, premium expectando.

Que Cristus legit reuoluto libro, pro se legit. Et pro eo uera [9]
erant, quia *spiritus domini* uere super eum erat, qui habuit omnem plenitudinem gratie, et ipse erat missus *ad ewangelizandum pauperibus*. Vnde ipse ait his qui erant in templo: *'Hodie impleta est hec scriptura in auribus uestris.' Et mirabantur omnes*, etc.

Per hoc quod Cristus legit distincte et aperte ad intelligendum [11]

16 8 *Significatiue non materialiter*: cf. *DMLBS* s.v. *significativus* 2b.
9 *spirituali*: i.e. the spiritual significance of scripture; see *DMLBS* s.v. *spiritalis* 6 and Solignac, 'L'apparition du mot *spiritualitas* au moyen âge,' 193 (cf. Peter the Chanter's usage of the word at 199–201.)
13–15 *die... liber*: Lc 4:16–17
21–23 *spiritus... pauperibus*: Lc 4:18
23–25 *Hodie... omnes*: Lc 4:21–22

16.8 significatiue *corr. in MS from* significa**** **16.10** uelut *corr. in MS from* uelud *by another hand*

Spiritus domini, etc., intelligitur quod lector distincte ad intelligendum et apertę legere debet, et spirituali gratia clarere, et sic aliis uerbum dei predicare.

Hec sunt uerba in Ysaia: *Spiritus domini super me, eo quod* [12] *unxerit me—ad ewangelizandum pauperibus misit me—ad annunciandum mansuetis misit me, ut mederer contritos corde et predicarem captiuis indulgentiam et clausis apertionem, ut predicarem annum placabilem domino et diem ultionis deo nostro, ut consolarer omnes lugentes, et ponerem fortitudinem lugentibus Syon, et darem eis coronam procinere, oleum gaudii pro luctu pallium, laudis pro spiritu meroris.*

⟨17⟩.

CIM CISSET NERVO distinguendo memorato:
Res aliquid multis dicitur esse modis.

Multipliter dicitur res esse aliquid. Per causam. *Tu es pacien-* [1–2] *tia mea domine*. Imitatione. Dixit Iesus disc⟨ipulis⟩ su⟨is⟩: *Vnus uestrum diabolus est*, id est imitatur diabolum; hoc dictum est pro Iuda. Methaforice. Dixit Iesus: *Ego sum uitis uera*. Per communione. *Predicate ewangelium omni creature*, id est homini, qui dicitur 'omnis creatura,' quia cum omni creatura habet aliquid commune; cum lapidibus et huiusmodi, esse; cum arboribus, uiuere; cum animalibus, sentire; cum angelis,

30–37 *Spiritus... meroris*: a conflation of Lc 4:18–19 and Is 61:1–3

17 3 *Multipliter = multipliciter* (cf. *tripliter* below, 50.28.)
3–4 *Tu... domine*: Ps 70:5
4–5 *Vnus... est*[1]: Io 6:71 (*uestrum* for Vulg. *ex uobis*)
6 *Ego sum uitis uera*: Io 15:1
7 *Predicate... creature*: Mc 16:15

16.27 etc intelligitur *written over eras. in original hand* **16.37** pallium *corr. in MS from* psallium **17** *the change in subject and metre here necessitates a new section; there is no indication of this in MS* **17.2** aliquid: *another hand adds* uel alicuiusmodi *above the line* **17.5** uestrum *corr. in MS from* imitat** **17.7** predicate ewangelium *corr. in MS from* predica** **17.8** omni *corr. in MS from* homini

discernere. Interpretatione. Cristus est Dauid; Dauid interpretatur 'manu fortis' siue 'aspectu desiderabilis.' Sicnificatione. *Petra erat Cristus*. Similitudine. Dixit Iesus de Iohanne: *Ipse est Helias*, scilicet similis Helie, quia ita ille precessit primum aduentum Cristi, sicut Helyas precedet secundum aduentum. Effectu. *Erat Iesus eiciens demonium et illud erat mutum*. Dicebatur 'mutum,' quia faciebat hominem mutum. Transubstantiatione. Dicit Paulus: *Probet se unusquisque et sic de pane illo edat*, etc. Sic intelligitur quod panis in altari est corpus Cristi transubstantiatione, quia transubstantiatur in corpus Cristi. Nuncupatiue. *Omnes dii gentium demonia*. Emphatice. *Quousque iusticia conuertitur in iudicium*, id est, Quousque iusti conuer⟨tunt⟩ in iu⟨dicium⟩. Resolutione. *Memento homo, quia cinis es; homo in cinerem resoluitur*. Veritate. Dixit Petrus Cristo: *Tu es filius dei uiui*. Officio. Episcopus quandoque dicitur sponsus ecclesie, quia est officialis et uicarius sponsi ecclesie, scilicet Cristi.

Per litteras harum trium dictionum—'cim,' 'cisset, 'neruo'—potest haberi in memoria distinctio facta hoc modo. Res dicitur esse aliquid:

11–12 *Interpretatione…desiderabilis*: also found in *Ex auditis super psalmos*, Ps 2:1 (fol. 9rb)
Dauid[2]*…desiderabilis*: this interpretation is used at a number of points in Peter Lombard, *Commentarium in Psalmos*, e.g. Ps. 2.intro (PL 191:69b); from Jerome, *Liber interpretationis hebraicorum nominum* 35 (CCSL 72:103, line 11).

13 *Petra erat Cristus*: 1 Cor 10:4

13–14 *Ipse est Helias*: Mt 11:14

15–16 *Helyas…aduentum*: cf. Mal 4:5.

16–17 *Erat…mutum*[1]: Lc 11:14

18–19 *Probet…edat*: 1 Cor 11:28

21 *Omnes…demonia*: Ps 95:5

22 *Quousque…iudicium*: Ps 93:15

23–24 *Memento…resoluitur*: used at the imposition of ashes on Ash Wednesday; cf. Gen 3:19 and below, 35.24–25.

25 *Tu es filius dei uiui*: Mt 16:16

25–26 *Episcopus…ecclesie*: cf. Peter the Chanter, *Verbum adbreuiatum*, textus alter 34 (CCCM 196b:175, lines 158–159).

17.25 episcopus *preceded by* q *in MS before corr.* (*scribe had begun to write* quandoque)

C Causa,	C Communione,	N Numcupatione,
I Imitatione,	I Interpretatione,	E Emphasi,
M Metaphoria,	S Significatione,	R Resolutione,
	S Similitudine,	V Veritate,
	E Effectu,	O Officio.
	T Transubstantiatione,	

18. De articulis in quibus licet uiro non reddere debita sponse

In quibus articulis liceat non reddere sponsis
Persoluenda thoro sponsis, per SCINDE notato.

Sex faciunt quod non tenetur uir reddere debitum uxori: suscitatio, corruptio, indignitas (scilicet fornicatio), necessitas, defectus, exemptio. Suscitatio, quia si quis suscitaretur ut Lazarus, non tenetur reddere debitum uxori, quia dicit Paulus: *Mortuo uiro, soluta est mulier. Nubat cui uoluerit.* Corruptio, quia sponsus metuens corruptionem propriam siue alienam licite potest non accedere ad uxorem cor⟨ruptam⟩ propriam—quia si metuit infectionem lepre, uxore habente lepram inficientem, potest licite non accedere ad eam, quod sic decreuit papa [2–3]

18 2–3 An extended version of this poem appears in William de Montibus, *Versarius*, under 'Matrimonium' (fol. 71r). Other versions are found in London, British Library, MS Harley 956, fol. 24r, edited by Dinkova-Bruun, 'Notes on Poetic Composition in the Theological Schools ca. 1200,' 320 (with note in introduction, 304) and in Alexander of Hales, *Glossa in quatuor libros Sententiarum Petri Lombardi* 4.31.16a (where it stands for *suspicio, corruptio, indignitas, necessitas, membri depositio, exemptio*).

3 *thoro* = *toro*

7–8 *Mortuo…mulier*: Rom 7:2, from Gratian, C.2 q.3 d.p. c.7. Cf. below, 39.185.

8 *Nubat cui uoluerit*: 1 Cor 7:39

12–13 *sic…Alexander*: this appears to be incorrect; cf. *Liber extra* 4.8.1. On this pope's marriage legislation, see Brundage, 'Marriage and Sexuality in the Decretals of Pope Alexander III.' Peter

18.3 per *corr. in MS from* p **18.4** faciunt *subst. for* faciumt *MS* **18.11** infectionem *corr. in MS from* effectionem **18.12** papa: *another hand adds* papa *in MS above the line, interpreting the original abbreviation as* propter

Alexander. Metuens quoque cor⟨reptam⟩ alienam, licite potest non accedere, scilicet quando mulier menstrua paritur, quia frequenter corrumpitur fetus conceptus tempore menstrui sanguinis. Moyses quodam loco iussit occidi uirum accedentem ad mulierem menstruatam. Alio loco iussit ut puniretur uel pena corporali uel pena pecuniaria. Indulgenda sunt hec diuersa precepta hoc modo: Si ignorans accederet, puniretur; si sciens, occideretur. Fornicatio quoque facit quod non tenetur uir accedere ad uxorem, quia si fornicatio probata fuerit, potest eam dimittere, sed non potest aliam ducere illa uiuente. Dicit Ieronimus quod etiam uehemens suspicio et probata facit quod potest uir licite non accedere ad uxorem. Spiritualis quoque fornicatio facit quod non tenetur uir reddere debitum uxori, scilicet si contingat quod ille sit conuersus ab infidelitate, et illa non uult conuerti. Necessitas similiter facit, etc., scilicet si sit incarceratus uel magna laborans egritudine. Defectus quoque facit, etc., scilicet si sit ementulatus. Exemptio quoque facit, etc., quia si iusta sententia dampnetur ad mortem, iudex potest eum tradere aliquibus claustralibus potentibus et ita eum eximere a potestate mulieris.

S Suscitatio, [2]
C Corruptio,
I Indignitas (scilicet fornicatio),
N Necessitas,
D Defectus,
E Exemptio.

---

the Chanter frequently mentions Alexander in his *Summa de sacramentis et animae consiliis*, and holds a view consistent with that of the pope at 3.29.274 (ed. Dugauquier, 3.2a:296, lines 22–27).

16–18 *Moyses…pecuniaria*: cf. Lev 15:33, 18:29, 20:18.

20–21 *quod…uxorem*: Gratian, C.32 q.1 c.2, quoting Jerome, *Commentarii in euangelium Matthaei* 3 (CCSL 77:167, lines 768–769)

27 *etc*: i.e. *quod non tenetur uir reddere debitum uxori*

29 *ementulatus*: 'emasculated' (*DMLBS* s.v. *ementulare*)

18.21 si *om. MS before corr.; add. above the line by another hand* **18.31** ita *subst. for* ira *MS*

19. De formis male iurandi

Si male iurandi formas sit mens memorandi, *98r*
Per primas FATO, per IDONEA commemorato.

Diuersis modis contingit male iurare. Ab aliquo iuratur falso, et [2–3] hoc prohibitum est. Vnde habetur in decalogo: *Non peierabis.* Ab aliquo iuratur appetitiue. Vnde Iacobus in epistula canonica ait: *Ante omnia, fratres mei, nolite iurare*, scilicet, Ne uelitis, ne appetatis iurare. Ab aliquo iuratur impetuose. Sic Dauid iurauit arrepto gladio cum impetu quod interficeret Nabal uirum stultum, sed postea reuocauit ensem. Ab aliquo iuratur dolose. Vnde in psalmo dicitur: *Nec iurauit in dolo proximo suo.* Ab aliquo otiose iuratur. Vnde dicitur: *Non accipies nomen dei tui in uanum.* Ab aliquo iuratur negligenter. Iosue, cui precepit dominus delere Gabaonitas, confederauit se Gabaonitis et iurauit eis et non consuluit os domini per Eleazar sicut preceptum erat illi, ut consuleret os domini per Eleazar de eis que essent facienda. Ab aliquo iuratur erronee ab eo, scilicet qui iurat per creaturas credendo aliquid numinis inesse eis, et ideo

19 2–3 These verses are earlier found in a sermon on *Qui non est mecum, contra me est* (Lc 14:16) attributed to Serlo of Wilton (ed. Braceland, 46, lines 125–126; introduction, xvi), with a slightly different first line ('Si male iurandi species sit cura notandi'). They also appear in William de Montibus, *Versarius*, under 'Iuramentum' (fol. 59v); in Alexander of Hales, *Glossa in quatuor libros Sententiarum* 3.39.28f; and in a fourteenth-century copy of Robert Grosseteste's *Templum domini*, London, British Library, Royal MS 8 D.IV, fol. 83r.

5 *Non peierabis*: Lev 19:12

6 *appetitiue*: 'out of desire' (*DMLBS* s.v. *appetitivus*)

7 *Ante…iurare*: Iac 5:12

8–10 *Dauid…ensem*: cf. 1 Sam 25:13–35.

11 *Nec…suo*: Ps 23:4

12–13 *Non…uanum*: Ex 20:7

13–14 *cui…Gabaonitas*: cf. Ios 9:24, Deut 7:1–2.

14–15 *confederauit…consuluit*: cf. Ios 9:14–15.

16–17 *ut…facienda*: cf. Num 27:21.

17 *erronee*: 'mistakenly' (*DMLBS* s.v. *erronee*)

19.1 de…iurandi *om. MS before corr.; add. in a slightly different hand* **19.4** iurare *subst. for* iurate *MS* **19.12** otiose *corr. in MS in a different ink from* ociose

esse uenerandas. Erronee quoque iurat qui per creaturas iurat et putat quod non teneatur soluere iuramentum. Sicut laudatur creator in creatura, ita iuratur creator in creatura. Ab aliquo iuratur assidue. Vnde dicitur: *Non usurpabis nomen dei tui in uanum*. 'Vsurpabis,' id est non in usum rapies. Et alibi dicitur: *Non assuescat os tuum iurationi*. Vbi ait dominus in ewangelio: *Ego autem dico non iurare omnino*, non prohibet iurare, quia ipse iurauit quando dixit Abrahe: *Per memet ipsum iuraui*, etc. Sed docuit non male iurare, scilicet falso, uel impetuose, uel appetitiue, uel dolose, uel ociose, uel negligenter, uel erronee, uel assidue.

F Falso, I Impetuose [2]
A Appetitiue, D Dolose,
T O Ociose,
O N Negligenter,
E Erronee,
A Assidue.

20. Hinc potest sumi exemplum fugiendi quandoque persecutionem

Cristus in Egyptum fugiens, sic esse fugandum
Sepius electum docet improbitate malorum.
Prebet et exemplum ne cui metuenda malorum
Sit rabies, licite fugiens cum possit abire.

Sicut Cristus fleuit Lazarum ut alios doceret habere caritatem [6]
erga proximos, et sicut orauit ut alios instrueret et formam

19–21 *Erronee...creatura*: cf. above, 7.11–13.
20–21 *Sicut...creatura*: this might be understood from Mt 23:21–22.
22–23 *Non...uanum*: Deut 5:11
24 *Non...iurationi*: Eccli 23:9
25 *Ego...omnino*: Mt 5:34
26 *Per memet ipsum iuraui*: Gen 22:16

20 3 *Cristus...fugiens*: cf. Mt 2:13–15.
7 *Cristus fleuit Lazarum*: Io 11:35; cf. 10.25–26, 30.16–17.
8–9 *orauit...daret*: i.e. in the Lord's Prayer: Lc 11:1–4, Mt 6:9–13

19.28 ociose: -c- *eras. in MS (probably with the intent of changing the word to* otiose *as above) but not replaced*

orandi daret, ita fugit ut aliis auferret inconsulte temeritatis audaciam.

21. De diuisione corporis Cristi super altare

Diuiditur partes caro Cristi pro tribus in tres.
  Partes catholica tres habet ecclesia:
Premia sunt patrie requiesque, triumphus; hic igne
  Et labor; inque uia pugna, labor, merita.

tribus: Scilicet pro tribus partibus uniuersalis ecclesie. [2]

Catholica ecclesia, id est uniuersalis ecclesia, habet ·iii· partes, scilicet ecclesiam militantem in uia, ecclesiam expectantem in igne purgatorio, ecclesiam triumphantem in patria. [3]

In ecclesia militante in uia est pugna, labor, meritum. In ecclesia triumphante in patria est triumphus, requies, premium. In ecclesia expectante in igne purgatorio est labor et triumphus. [4–5]

hic: Scilicet triumphus. [4]
igne: Purgatorio.

22. Hic docetur discretio fugiendi in heremum siue in aliquod claustrum

Si deserta petis, non sit dux aura fauoris;
Huc sis expulsus seu ductus quo duce Cristus.

deserta: Id est herenum uel quodcumque claustrum. [3]

Vnus ewangelista dicit: *Ductus est Iesus in desertum a spiritu*, etc. Alius dicit: *Cum ascendisset de aqua*, scilicet post baptismum, *expulit eum spiritus in desertum*, etc. [4]
quo: Scilicet spiritu sancto.

22 1 *heremum*: used to refer to both the desert and a hermitage or monastery (*DMLBS* s.v. *eremus*)
6 *Ductus…spiritu*: Mt 4:1
7 *Cum…aqua*: a common paraphrase of Mc 1:10
8 *expulit…desertum*: Mc 1:12

23. Hic notatur quod peccatum commissum aliud attrahit

Non scandit montem Loth habens incredulitatem 98v
Incestumque, speciem, commisit ob ebrietatem.

Loth egresso a Sodoma precepit angelus ut ascenderet montem; [2–3] sed ipse, non credens se esse tutum in monte, non adquieuit angelo sed habitauit in Segor. Et post incredulitatem incurrit ebrietatem. Et post ebrietatem incurrit incestum, quia illo inebriato filie eius eo nesciente conceperunt de eo. Ex his intelligi potest quod unum peccatum est causa efficiens alterius peccati. In monte dicuntur esse qui in martyrio sunt, et qui in uirginitate sunt, et qui in heremo sunt, et qui in contemptu mundi sunt. Et coniugati in monte dicuntur esse, si non carnali uoluptate soluuntur, sed causa prolis suscipiende ⟨conceperunt⟩.

commisit: Turpitudo latebras querit. [3]

24. Hic notantur quedam que predicatorem congruit obseruare

Strenuus ut Cristus, sis utilis atque benignus.
Hic loca circuiens docuit bona, morbida curans
Vtque bone fame fuerat. Sic te decet esse.

In ewangelio dicitur quod Cristus *circuibat Galileam predicando*, [3–5] et ex hoc quod ita strenuus erat, docuit predicatores debere esse strenuos, et docuit *ewangelium regni*, scilicet

23 3 *Incestumque speciem*: *incestus* was understood as a *species libidinis*, *fornicationis*, or *luxurie*.
4–6 *Loth…Segor*: cf. Gen 19:17–22.
7–8 *Et…eo*[2]: cf. Gen 19:30–36.
13 *causa…conceperunt*: cf. Peter Lombard, *Sententiae* 4.31.7.4, quoting Augustine: 'prolis suscipiendae causa utrumque sexum commiscent.'

24 6–8 *circuibat…regni*: Mt 4:23 (cf. above, 11.25.)

23.3 speciem *subst. for* specii *MS* **23.9** unum *corr. in MS from* u*um **24.4** bona *corr. in MS from* bna **24.7** predicatores *corr. in MS from* predicaretores

ewangelium quod ducit regnum. In hoc ostendit quod predicator utilis esse debet bona predicando: Et dum predicauit, *curauit languidos*. In hoc ostendit quod benignus debet esse predicator: Et dum predicauit, creuit eius bona opinio. In hoc ostensum est quod predicator debet esse bone fame, que necessaria est ei propter proximos.

loca: Scilicet diuersa loca Galilee. [4]
bona: Scilicet ewangelium regni.
morbida: Scilicet diuersos languidos.

25. De scandalo uitando

Que mala sunt in eis, que nec mala nec bona sunt his:
Scandala uitabis semper. Sed que bona sunt his:
Cum non precipua sint hec, tu scandala uita;
Cum sint precipua, tunc abice scandala cura.
Non sint in cura tibi tristia scandala salua
Vite, iusticie, doctrine, comoditate.

In mal⟨is⟩ et in indifferentibus semper uitanda sunt scandala. [2–5]
In bonis etiam uitandum est scandalum, cum non sint precipua. Dicitur enim: *Ve homini, per quem scandalum uenit.*

Salua triplice ueritate non est curandum de scandalo: ueritate [6–7]
uite, quantum ad quemlibet; ueritate iusticie, quantum ad iudicem; ueritate doctrine, quantum ad predicatorem. Cristus in quibusdam de scandalo non curauit, quia multi in uerbo eius scandalizati sunt cum dixit: *Nisi manducaueritis carnem filii hominis et biberitis eius sanguinem, non habetis uitam in uobis.*

11 *curauit languidos*: Mt 14:14
12 *creuit eius bona opinio*: cf. Mt 4:24.

25 10 *Ve…uenit*: Mt 18:7
11–20 *Salua…cecorum*: cf. a greatly expanded version of the same ideas in Peter the Chanter, *Summa de sacramentis et animae consiliis* 3.45.319 (ed. Dugauquier, 3.2a:376–377, lines 20–61).
15–16 *Nisi…uobis*: Io 6:54

25.4 sint *corr. in MS from* sunt **25.13** predicatorem *corr. in MS from* predicato*** **25.14** scandalo *subst. for* scandolo *MS*

Scandalizati sunt etiam multi cum dixit: *Quod intrat in os hominis in uentrem uadit et in secessum emittitur*, etc. Vnde: *Discipuli dixerunt ei, Scis quia pharisei scandalizati sunt in uerbo isto?* Et dixit eis: *Sinite eos; ceci sunt et duces cecorum.*

26. Hic datur intelligi qualiter Cristianus uero crismate debet inungi

Balsama conficias oleo, te talibus ungas. *99r*
Sic aliis redole; sic tibi mente nite.

Cristianus crismate inunctus est. Et ut uere sit Cristianus, debet [3] habere suauitatem serenate conscientie et sinceritatem fame, et sic erit unctus uero crismate. Crisma conficitur ex oleo et balsamo. Per oleum accipitur nitor et suauitas serenate conscientie, que necessaria est homini propter se ipsum. Per balsamum quod est odoriferum accipitur sinceritas fame que est necessaria homini propter proximum.

aliis: Scilicet ad utilitatem aliorum, [4]
redole: per bonam famam.
tibi: Scilicet ad utilitatem tui ipsius,
nite: per bonam conscientiam.

17–18 *Quod…emittitur*: Mt 15:17. The addition of *hominis* is later found in Thomas of Chobham, *Summa de arte praedicandi* 4 (CCCM 82:116, line 888).
18–19 *Discipuli…isto*: Mt 15:12 (*in uerbo isto* for Vulg. *audito uerbo*)
20 *Sinite…cecorum*: Mt 15:14

26 5–11 *Cristianus[1]…proximum*: reused below, 39.41–46
6 *serenate conscientie*: the use of these words together appears to have originated in the twelfth century, perhaps with Bernard of Clairvaux, *Sermones super Cantica Canticorum* 57.8 (ed. Leclercq, Talbot, and Rochais, 2:124, line 8) or Peter the Venerable, *Epistulae* 53 (ed. Constable, 1:165); see also Peter the Chanter, *Verbum adbreuiatum*, textus prior 5 (CCCM 196a:41, line 14); textus alter 47 (CCCM 196b:251, lines 100–101); for later usage, see *DMLBS* s.v. *serenare* 2b.

25.17 os *corr. in MS from* hos **25.19** ei *corr. in MS from* ci | pharisei *corr. in MS from* multi *by another hand* **26.10** odoriferum *corr. in MS from* odoferum *by another hand*

27. Hic habetur qualiter hoc nomen 'panis' in plerisque scripturis accipiatur

Diuersos queres a celesti patre panes;
Hos ex SCOPE DOCES ('o' dempta) concipe panes.

[4] Est panis corporalis substantie, de quo dicitur: *Frange esurienti panem tuum*, in quo attenditur quod debes frangere et dare partem, si non possis totum dare; et esurienti dare debes, quia uasa uacua implenda sunt et non plena. Est panis operationis bone, de quo dicitur: *Cybus meus est ut faciam uoluntatem patris mei*. Est panis penitentie, de quo dicitur: *Fuerunt mihi lacrime mee panis die ac nocte*. Et alibi dicitur: *Surgite postquam sederitis qui manducatis panem doloris*. Panis doloris est panis penitentie, quem manducans, penitens, sedere debet, scilicet humiliare se et postea surgere. Designatus quoque fuit panis penitentie per panem quem fecit Abraham coquere sub cinere, et apposuit angelis quos inuitauit ad ospicium, credens illos homines esse. Et bene panis subcinericeus—per quem designatur pa⟨nis⟩ penitentie—appositus est angelis, quia gaudium est angelis dei super peccatore penitentiam agente. Designatusque est pa⟨nis⟩ pe⟨nitentie⟩ per panem subcinericium quem euigilans Helias inuenit ad capud suum, et precepit ei angelus ut comederet. Et comedit, et iterum dormiuit, et dixit ei iterum angelus: *Surge et comede*.

27 5–6 *Frange…tuum*: Is 58:7
6 *attenditur quod*: 'it is noted that' (*DMLBS* s.v. *attendere* 3c)
8 *uasa…plena*: cf. Peter of Blois, *Carmina* 1.3.2.21–22 (CCCM 128:253).
9–10 *Cybus…mei*: Io 4:34 (*patris mei* for Vulg. *eius qui misit me;* cf. Mt 7:21 and 12:50.)
10–11 *Fuerunt…nocte*: Ps 41:4
11–12 *Surgite…doloris*: Ps 126:2
15–17 *panem…esse*: cf. Gen 18:2–6.
17 *ospicium = hospitium*
17–18 *subcinericeus*: 'baked beneath hot ashes' (*DMLBS* s.v. *subcinericius*), from Gen 18:6
21–25 *panem…diebus*: 3 Reg 19:5–8

27.4 hos *subst. for* hoc *MS* **27.16** cinere *subst. for* cineree *MS*

Et surrexit et comedit iterum. Et cibo illo conualescens, iuit usque ad montem Sina. Et fuit in illo itinere ·xl· diebus. Hoc cibo, id est cibo penitentie, fit homo ualidus; et hoc cibo debet pluries uesci, ut conualescat ad iter peragendum. Est panis sancte eucharistie, de quo dicit dominus: *Ego sum panis uiuus qui de celo descendi*. Hic panis digne sumptus mentem refrigerat ab estu carnalis concupiscentie et ducit ad uitam eternam. Est panis dilectionis siue caritatis, de quo dicitur: *Si quis petit patrem panem, numquid lapidem dabit illi?*, id est, Si petit caritatem, numquid dabit illi duriciam odii? Sicut omnis mensa inops est sine pane, ita bona opera meritoria non sunt uite eterne si desit caritas. Est panis cognitionis, de quo dicitur: *Beatus homo qui manducabit panem in regno patris mei*. Est panis eloquii sacri, unde dicitur: 'Erant ·xii· panes propositionis in mensa tabernaculi.' Mistice dicuntur ibi panes doctrine apostolice in sacra scriptura. Et pro Adam dictum est in psalmo: *Percussus sum ut fenum et aruit cor meum, quia oblitus sum comedere panem meum*. Adam percussus est et aruit tamquam fenum, necessitati mortis addictus, quando egit contra sacrum uerbum dei, quo prohibitus erat comedere de pomo, et uisus est oblitus comedere panem suum, scilicet memorare sacrum uerbum dei.

Est panis

S	Substantie et est pa⟨nis⟩	D	Dilectionis,
C	Corporalis,	O	
O	Operationis,	C	Cognit⟨i⟩onis,
P	Penitentie,	E	Eloquii
E	Eucharistie,	S	Sacri.

28–29 *Ego…descendi*: Io 6:51
32–33 *Si…illi*: Lc 11:11
36–37 *Beatus…mei*: a rephrasing of Lc 14:15
38–39 *Erant…scriptura*: *Glosa marg.* to Lev 24:5, quoting Bede, *De tabernaculo* 1 (CCSL 119a:27, line 878)
40–42 *Percussus…meum*: Ps 101:5

27.32 lapidem *corr. in MS from* labidem **27.35** desit *corr. in MS from* desi **27.48** dilectionis *subst. for* dilelctionis *MS*

28. Hic datur intelligi qualiter hec nomina ‘sinistra,’ ‘dextera’ solent accipi

Quid fiat dextra non debet scire sinistra. *99v*
Prudens in dextra cor habet stultusque sinistra.

Dominus in ewangelio—ubi dicit: *Nesciat sinistra quid faciat* [3–4] *dextra*—prius agit de operatione bona, postea de oratione, et post⟨ea⟩ de ieiunio, et postea de intentione. Et ita notatur q⟨uo⟩d parum prosunt operat⟨i⟩o, oratio, et ieiunium, nisi fiant cum bona intentione. Quandoque dicitur ‘dextera’ fauor, ut ibi: *In potestatibus salus dextere eius*, id est salus fauoris eius. Alibi dicitur: *Delectationes in dextera tua usque in finem*, id est in fauore tuo. Quandoque dicitur ‘dextera’ nimius rigor iusticie sicut et ‘sinistra’ nimia remissio. Vnde illud: *Nec declinabis ad dextram neque ad sinistram*, id est, Non eris nimis rigidus et seuerus in iusticia facienda neque nimis remissus. ‘Medium tenuere beati.’ Quandoque dicitur ‘dextra’ uirtus, et ‘sinistra’ uicium. Vnde illud: *Nesciat sinistra quid faciat dextra*, id est, Non admilceat se uicium operi uirtutis. Quandoque dicitur ‘dextra’ prosperitas et ‘sinistra’ aduersitas. Dicit apostolus: *Per arma iusticie a dextris et a sinistris*, scilicet armati debemus esse in prosperis, ne extollamur; in aduersis, ne deprimamur. Quandoque dicitur ‘dextera’ eterna beatitudo: *Considerabam ad dexteram, et uidebam, et non erat qui cognosceret me*, id est attendebam ad eternam beatitudinem, et uidebam, et tunc alii non nouerunt me, reputantes me stultum et delirum.

28 5–6 *Nesciat…dextra*: Mt 6:3
9–10 *In…eius*[1]: Ps 19:7 (Vulg. *potentatibus*)
11 *Delectationes…finem*: Ps 15:10
13–14 *Nec…sinistram*: Deut 17:11
16 *Medium tenuere beati*: Walther, *Proverbia*, no. 14571; also used in Peter the Chanter, *Verbum adbreuiatum*, textus conflatus 1.66 (CCCM 196:437, line 16; 439, line 74); textus prior 60 (CCCM 196a:378, line 12); textus alter 52 (CCCM 196b:267, line 135)
17–18 *Nesciat…dextra*: Mt 6:3
18 *admilceat = admulceat*, ‘flatter’
20 *Per…sinistris*: 2 Cor 6:7
22–24 *Considerabam…me*: Ps 141:5

28.18 quandoque *corr. in MS from* quando

Sic Martinus, habens uultum erectum ad celum et attendens ad eter⟨nam⟩ bea⟨titudinem⟩, senex delirus reputabatur a quibusdam. Alibi dicitur: *Separabit oues ab edis, et oues statuet ad dextram et edos ad sinistram*, scilicet bonos ducet ad eternam beatitudinem, malos mittet ad eternam dampnationem.

[3] Id est non debet uicium admisceri operi uirtutis, quia *modicum fermenti totam massam corrumpit.*

[4] Quandoque per 'dextram' accipiuntur bona spiritualia, et per 'sinistram' bona temporalia. Vnde dicitur: *Cor sapientis in dextra, cor stulti in sinistra.*

29. De oratione

Non prece deuota phariseus, ypocrita, scriba
Orat. Non ora sic pro questu neque pompa,
Nec triplici causa multis uelut ennicus ora
Verbis. Vt Cristus precibus prolixius usus,
Noctu mente bona, sic tu prolixius ora.

[2–3] Non debet oratio esse questuosa; cuiusmodi orationem faciebant scribe et pharisei. Vnde dicitur: *Ve uobis scribe et pharisei qui deuoratis domos uiduarum sub obtentu prolixe orationis*. Nec debet oratio esse pomposa siue laudis appeti-

26–28 *Martinus…quibusdam*: cf. Bernard of Clairvaux, *Sermo in festo sancti Martini* 14 (ed. Leclercq and Rochais, 5:409, lines 13–15) and Peter the Chanter, *Verbum adbreuiatum*, textus conflatus 1.88 (CCCM 196:602, lines 10–12); textus alter 89 (CCCM 196b:447, lines 25–26). *Ad habendum memoriam*, Bodley 860, fol. 153r, cites the life of Martin in Sulpicius Severus, epist. 3 (ed. J. Fontaine): there is not a specific textual reference here, but see 3.10 and 3.18.

28–29 *Separabit…sinistram*: a paraphrase of Mt 25:32–33

31–32 *modicum…corrumpit*: 1 Cor 5:6; Gal 5:9

34–35 *Cor…sinistra*: Eccl 10:2

29 8–10 *Ve…orationis*: a conflation of Mt 23:14 and Mc 12:40, also found in Gerald of Wales, *Gemma ecclesiastica* 1.49 (ed. Brewer, 132)

29.4 uelut *corr. in MS from* uelud **29.10–11** siue…appetitiua *om. MS before corr.; add. in marg. by another hand*

tiua; cuiusmodi orationi insistunt ypocrite, qui dicuntur orare *in angulis platearum*. Per hoc quod dicitur, 'in angulis,' innuitur quod appetunt uideri nolle apparere. Per hoc quod dicitur, 'platearum,' in quibus fit multorum transitus, innuitur quod appetunt non omnino latere.

Non prohibetur quis orare prolixe, quia Cristus prolixe orauit [4–5]
quando in oratione pernoctauit, sed non debet quis uti multiloquiis orando eo modo quo ennici, id est gentiles, qui utebantur multiloquiis triplici de causa: propter instructionem, scilicet ut instruerent deos suos, id est demones quid peterent; et propter absentiam demonum quos putabant abesse cum non exaudiebantur; et propter persuasionem, quia credebant multis persuasionibus demones mouere ad id faciendum quod peterent. 'Ennos' Grece, 'gentiles' Latine. Inde 'ennicus,' scilicet gentilis. Huiusmodi oratio que fit mente bona est oratio caritatiua. Quedam oratio est timida, que non procedit. Quedam est tepida, que in uia deficit. Quedam est temeraria, que peruenit sed repulsa resilit.

30. De ieiunio

Ex FACIE memora quod sunt ieiunia plura;
Quod designat 'c' generale uel est speciale. *100r*

Ieiunium fastidientis est quando aliquis ieiunat ut ita irritet gu- [2]
lam ad maiorem appetitum comedendi. Hoc ieiunium non est

12 *in angulis platearum*: Mt 6:5
17 *oratione pernoctauit*: cf. Lc 6:12.
18 *ennici = ethnici;* on its medieval use as an equivalent to *pagani*, see Stotz, *Handbuch*, 3:11–12 (V § 3.10).
24 *Ennos* = ἔθνος, 'nation, people' (cf. ἐθνικός, 'gentile').

30 2 *Ex…plura*: this verse also appears in William de Montibus, *Versarius*, under 'Ieiunium' (fol. 60r).
3 *c*: scan *cē*, rhyming with *speciale*; cf. below, 50.3.
4–17 *Ieiunium…careat*: cf. Peter the Chanter, *Verbum adbreuiatum*, textus conflatus 2.42 (CCCM 196:754–755, lines 11–30); textus prior 121 (CCCM 196a:623–624, lines 15–18); textus alter 97 (CCCM 196b:462, lines 5–18).

29.18 ennici *subst. for* eunici *MS* **29.28** resilit *corr. in MS from* resili

meritorium; hoc ieiunium est de scola Epic⟨uri⟩. Ieiunium auari est quando aliquis ieiunat ut sua non minuat. Qui ita ieiunat, ieiunat marsupio. Hoc ieiunium non ualet. Ieiunium Cristiani est quando aliquis ex caritate ieiunat. Istud ieiunium bonum est. Ieiunium ypocrite est quando aliquis appetit uideri ab hominibus ieiunare. Qui sic ieiunat, ieiunat inani glorie. Et hoc ie⟨iunium⟩ non ualet. Ieiunium egri est quando aliquis ieiunat ut sanitatem recuperet. Hoc ie⟨iunium⟩ est de scola Ypocratis; hoc est ieiunium indifferens. Alicui ualet, illi scilicet qui desiderat sanitatem ut conualescens deo seruiat. Alicui non prodest hoc ie⟨iunium⟩, illi scilicet qui non appetit hac intentione sanitatem ut deo seruiat, sed ut dolore careat. Est ieiunium

F Fastidientis, et est ie⟨iunium⟩
A Auari,
C Cristiani,
I Ypocrite,
E Egri.

Duplex est ieiunium Cristiani: generale et speciale. Generale [3]
est quando et exterior homo et interior ieiunat, scilicet quando subtrahuntur uicia, sicut cibus et potus subtrahitur. Quidam designans generale ieiunium ait:

> Sit simul exclusus cum carne libidinis usus,
> Vtque cibum denti sic subtrahe crimina menti.

Speciale ie⟨iunium⟩ est quando homo abstinet a cibo et potu et facit opera misericordie; non tamen abstinet a uiciis.
c: Scilicet ieiunium Cristiani.

27–28 *Sit...menti*: Walther, *Initia*, no. 18331. To his sources may be added London, Lambeth Palace Library, MS 373, fol. 84v, where these verses (the second line reading 'Vtque cibum denti sic carnem subtrahe') are added to a copy of Smaragdus of Saint-Mihiel's *Diadema monachorum*. Oxford, Bodleian Library, MS Digby 104 (*SC* 1705), fol. 138vb, a poetic miscellany written in the late twelfth or early thirteenth century, provides the following text:

> Sit simul exclusus cum carne libidinis usus
> Atque cibum denti: sic crimina detrahe menti.
> Si duo conueniunt ieiunia, tunc bene fiunt
> Que nequeunt uere domino diuisa placere.

30.6 epicuri: *final letters eras. but not replaced in MS* **30.14** alicui *corr. in MS from* a**** **30.20** cristiani: *this is the only instance of* crist- *written unabbreviated in MS*

31. De intentione

Si fuerit simplex intentio, si plica duplex
Error et hinc praua sit delectatio pulsa,
Congeries operum clarescet tota tuorum.
Si nequam fuerit oculus, non illa nitebit.

Intentio debet esse sine duplici plica, sine plica erroris que [2–4]
tollit directionem ad debitum finem et sine plica praue delectationis que tollit debitum finem. Secundum hoc dicitur: *Si oculus tuus fuerit simplex, totum corpus tuum lucidum erit*, id est si intentio fuerit sine duplici plica, tota congeries operum illuminabitur. Intentio quorumdam Iudeorum qui crucifixerunt Cristum fuit sine plica praue delectationis, quia putabant se obsequium prestare deo; sed non fuit sine plica erroris. Dicitur quod 'intentio nomen operi imponit,' quia si intentio careat duplici plica, bonum est opus. 'Intentio' dicitur quasi 'in aliud tentio,' et ita hoc nomen 'intentio' duo complectitur: finem et directionem ad finem.

Dicitur: *Si oculus tuus*, id est intentio tua, *fuerit nequam, totum* [5]

31 6–11 *Intentio… illuminabitur*: cf. Peter the Chanter, *Verbum adbreuiatum*, textus conflatus 2.37 (CCCM 196:744, lines 29–30); textus alter 92 (CCCM 196b:456, lines 29–31).

6 *plica*[1]: 'fold,' 'ply' (*DMLBS* s.v. *plica* 1c)

8–9 *Si… erit*: Mt 6:22 or Lc 11:34 (cf. lines 18–19.)

8–11 *Si… illuminabitur*: cf. Peter the Chanter, *Summa de sacramentis et animae consiliis* 3.60.364 (ed. Dugauquier, 3.2b:535, lines 98–99); Simon of Tournai, *Disputationes* 41 (ed. Warichez, 120, lines 23–25).

14 *intentio… imponit*: Ambrose, *De officiis* 1.30.147 (CCSL 15:53, line 31), perhaps via Peter Lombard, *Sententiae* 2.40.2 and 2.40.12; also quoted with *intentio* for *adfectus* in Peter the Chanter, *Summa de sacramentis et animae consiliis* 3.60.364 (ed. Dugauquier, 3.2b:532, line 36)

15–16 *Intentio… tentio*: cf. Peter the Chanter, *Summa de sacramentis et animae consiliis* 3.60.364 (ed. Dugauquier, 3.2b:531, lines 19–20).

16 *tentio*: i.e. 'direction' (*DMLBS* s.v. *1 tensio* 2)

18–19 *Si… erit*: Mt 6:23; cf. Lc 11:34.

31.4 tuorum *corr. in MS from* duorum **31.15** bonum est *corr. in MS from* bon*e

corpus tuum tenebrosum erit. Plus dicitur, et minus significatur, id est, Nullum opus tuum erit meritorium uite eterne.
oculus: Id est intentio.
illa: Id est congeries operum.

32. De significatione horum nominum: seraph, cherub, seraphin, cherubin, seraphim, cherubim

Ordine maiori seraph et cherub inferiori
Quemque notat. Neutrum seraphin, cherubinque neutrum
Insimul acceptos, seraphim, cherubim quoque lectos
Quotlibet: 'm' finis primi generis datur istis.

In regione spirituum dicuntur esse tres gerarchie. 'Gerarchia' [3–6] dicitur a 'geras,' quod est sacer, et 'archos,' quod est princeps. Inde 'gerarchia,' id est 'sacer principatus.' In prima gerarchia inferiori sunt uirtutes, angeli, archangeli. In secunda sunt potestates, principatus, dominationes. In tercia sunt throni, cherubin, et seraphin. Et quia dicitur: *Omnia fac secundum exemplar quod tibi monstratum est in monte*, in ecclesia militante leguntur primo simul tres lectiones, et secundo simul tres, et tercio tres simul, ut illa imitetur in quo potest ecclesiam triumphantem in qua sunt ·ix· ordines angelorum. In superiori ordine angelorum quilibet angelus dicitur 'seraph,' et omnes insimul collecti

19 *Plus...significatur*: a phrase occasionally used to indicate synecdoche, as early as Pompeius, *Commentum artis Donati* (ed. Keil, 307, lines 34–35); or alternatively litotes, in the tradition of Servius, *Commentarius in Vergilii Aeneidos libros* 12.143 (ed. Thilo, 2:592, lines 4–5)

32 7 *gerarchie = hierarchiae*

7–9 *Gerarchia...principatus*: this etymology is very similar to that later used in Guillaume Durand, *Rationale diuinorum officiorum* 4.33.31 (CCCM 140:408, lines 279–281).

8 *geras* = ἱερός, 'holy'
archos = ἀρχός, 'leader'; cf. Peter Lombard, *Sententiae* 4.24.17.1

9–12 *In...seraphin*: cf. Peter Lombard, *Sententiae* 2.9.1.

12–13 *Omnia...monte*: a conflation of Hebr 8:5 and Ex 25:40

31.22 id est *om. MS before corr.* **32.2** seraphim *corr. in MS from* seraphin

'seraphin'; et 'seraphin' est neutri generis. Quotlibet in illo ordine, scilicet duo uel tres uel quatuor insimul collecti, dicuntur 'seraphim,' et 'seraphim' est masculini generis. In ordine inferiori illo ordine qui dicitur 'seraphin,' quilibet dicitur 'cherub,' et omnes insimul collecti dicuntur 'cherubin,' et 'cherubin' est neutri generis. Quotlibet in illo ordine, scilicet duo uel ·iii· uel quatuor insimul collecti, dicuntur 'cherubim,' et 'cherubim' est masculini generis.

33. In his monemur peccata cauere et comissa cito relinquere, quia mora in his maius attrahit periculum

Propter sex caueas peccata citoque relinquas. *100v*
Sex a te tolles: hec si bene tollere cures.
Sex per CHAME PIE memora; ·vi· cetera prime
IECIT EO PREDE faciant te mente tenere.

Cauere debet homo peccata, et que habet cito relinquere, ne [3] incidat in consuetudinem peccandi, quia hec firmiter ligat et premit. Hec significata est per lapidem sub qua Lazarus iam quadriduanus fetebat, et non potuit surgere nisi prius sublato lapide per manus aliorum. Sic peccator qui incidit in consuetudi nem peccandi non per se sed per alios surgit. Dicitur in psalmo: *Caro sunt, spiritus uadens et non rediens.* 'Vadens' in peccatum per se, 'et non rediens' per se. Cum magna autem difficultate surgit qui incidit in consuetudinem peccandi, quod intelligitur per hoc quod Cristus ad suscitationem Lazari lacrimatus est et infremuit spiritu. Debet etiam homo cauere peccata et cito ea relinquere propter accumulationem peccatorum, quia unum peccatum aliud adducit. Dicit propheta: *Sanguis sanguinem*

33 9–10 *lapidem…fetebat*: cf. Io 11:39.
10 *quadriduanus*: 'for four days,' used especially with reference to Lazarus (*DMLBS* s.v. *quadriduanus* 2b)
13 *Caro…rediens*: Ps 77:39
16–17 *Cristus…spiritu*: Io 11:33–35; cf above, 10.25–26, 20.7.
19–20 *Sanguis sanguinem tetigit*: Os 4:2

32.18 seraphin² *corr. in MS from* seraphim **32.20–21** inferiori *corr. in MS from* interiori **33.1** cauere *subst. for* canere *MS* **33.5** chame: *the scribe moved* -e *in MS to space the letters of this word more evenly*

tetigit, id est peccatum additum est peccato. Sicut gutta sanguinis exiens aliam attrahit, ita peccatum aliud attrahit. Debet etiam homo cauere et relinquere cito peccata propter mortem subitaneam, quia post mortem nulla est redemptio; post hanc non potest homo mereri siue demereri. Vnde in ewangelio dicitur de malo: *Ligans manibus et pedibus, mittite eum in tenebras exteriores*. Per manus accipiuntur opera, per pedes affectus. Post mortem ligantur manus et pedes, quia nec per opera nec per affectus mereri potest homo post mortem. Debet etiam homo cauere peccata et cito relinquere propter egritudinem, quia cum sit in egritudine propter anxietatem et morbi aggrauationem, non potest reducere ad memoriam peccata ut ea confiteatur et accipiat penitentiam, et propter nimiam anxietatem cicius querit medicum corporis quam medicum anime. Debet etiam homo ca⟨uere⟩ pec⟨cata⟩ et cito re⟨linquere⟩ propter ignem purgatorium, qui grauis est pena his qui multum peccauerunt, et non peregerunt hic penitentiam. Dicit Augus⟨tinus⟩ de igne purgatorio: Nulla pena in mundo tanta est, nec excogitari potest tanta; quanta est pena purgata. Debet etiam homo ca⟨uere⟩ pec⟨cata⟩ et ci⟨to⟩ re⟨linquere⟩ propter nimiam erubescentiam, scilicet ne tandem erubescat confiteri peccata cum multa fuerint et cum in eis aliquamdiu se sordidauerit.

sex: Scilicet propter consuetudinem peccandi, et accumulationem peccatorum, et mortem subitaneam, et egritudinem, et ignem purgatorium, et nimiam erubescentiam.

[4] Quidam elati sunt de peccatis, sicut aliquis homicida, qui estimat se magne probitatis, quia occidit hominem, et aliquando iactat se occidisse hominem (et multi fallaces iactant), aliquando se mala fecisse (sicut quidam mercatores et uenditores

23 *post[1]...redemptio*: cf. Peter the Chanter, *Verbum adbreuiatum*, textus conflatus 2.57 (CCCM 196:834, line 87); textus prior 135 (CCCM 196b:683, line 81).

25–26 *Ligans...exteriores*: Mt 22:13; *ligans* is likely an error for Vulg. *ligatis*.

31 *reducere ad memoriam*: 'to call to mind' (*DMLBS* s.v. *reducere* 2)

37–38 *Nulla...purgata*: cf. Peter Lombard, *Sententiae* 4.21.3.

33.20 sicut *corr. in MS from* sic **33.31** non *corr. in MS from* hec

mercium cum aliquos deluserint). Quidam etiam iuuenes elati sunt ex hoc quod puellas deluserunt et aliquando iactant se illas delusisse. Hi firmius ligantur peccatis, quia habent elationem et iactanciam de peccatis. Quidam querunt excusationem et operationem in peccatis. Adam et Eua, cum peccassent, absconderunt se et operuerunt se foliis, et excusationem precedebant peccato suo, quia cum dominus quesisset ab Adam quare sic fecisset, dixit: *Mulier quam dedisti mihi decepit me.* Et cum quesisset ab Eua quare sic fecisset, dixit: *Serpens decepit me.* In psalmo dicitur: *Verba iniquorum preualuerunt super nos*, scilicet, Verba Ade et Eue excusantia peccata preualuerunt super nos, quia multi, sicut Adam et Eua, pretendunt excusationem peccato suo. Debet igitur homo, qui uult mundari a peccatis, cauere sibi de excusatione et operatione peccatorum suorum. Quidam iacentes in peccatis habent presumptionem et blandiuntur sibi de misericordia dei, et promittunt sibi impunitatem. Quidam habent desperationem sicut Chaim qui dixit: *Maior est iniquitas mea quam ut ueniam merear.* Debet igitur homo cauere sibi ne presumat uel desperet.
sex: Scilicet iactantiam, elationem, excusationem, oper⟨a⟩tionem, presumptionem, desperationem.

sex: Scilicet hec ·vi·: [5]

C	Consuetudinem,	P	Purgatorium
H		I	Ignem,
A	Accumulat⟨i⟩onem,	E	Erubescentiam.
M	Mortem,		
E	Egritudinem,		

prime: Littere.

52–53 *Quidam…peccatis*: cf. Ps 140:4.
53–54 *absconderunt…foliis*: cf. Gen 3:7–8 (cf. below, 46.17–18.)
56 *Mulier…me*: Adam's response from Gen 3:12 is completed with the words of Eve: this is also found in Bernard of Clairvaux, *Sententiae* 3.107 (ed. Leclercq and Rochais, 6.2:174, lines 12–14) and Thomas of Chobham, *Sermones* 1 and 6 (CCCM 82a:12, line 320; 72, lines 281–282).
57 *Serpens decepit me*: Gen 3:13
58 *Verba…nos*: Ps 64:4
65–66 *Maior…merear*: Gen 4:13

33.52 iactanciam *corr. in MS from* iactanciamtionem

Scilicet hec ·vi·: [6]

I Iactantiam, E Excusat⟨i⟩onem, PRE Presumpt⟨i⟩onem,
E Elationem, O Operat⟨i⟩onem, DE Desperationem.
CIT

34. Hic notatur quare deus differat liberare aliquos in afflictione laborantes

Sepe laboranti differt deus auxiliari
Vt sic optatum post afflictum mage gratum
Fiat, et inde magis humilis caro pulsa flagellis
Fiat, et hinc humili purgatio plenior illi. *101r*

Deus differt quandoque liberare laborantem ut maior sit afflicti humiliatio, et ut plenior fiat illi purgatio, et ut gratior sit tandem facta liberatio. [3–6]

optatum: Scilicet salus optata. [4]

35. De colliriis oculorum cordis

Que bona sunt oculis cordis colliria, si uis
Noscere, mente FVIT habeas primasque POPOSCIT.

Multiplex est collirium quod illuminat oculos interiores, quia est collirium fidei, unde dicitur: *Fide purificans corda eorum*. Et est collirium humilitatis. Dicit Balaam: *Qui cadit uidet*, id est, Qui humiliat se illuminatur. Est et collirium ut per zelum. Hoc ita turbat oculum ad horam ut post limpidius uideat. Zelus quandoque dicitur feruor amoris. Est et collirium tribulationis. Fel piscis aperuit oculos Thobie: per hoc datur intelligi quod amara tribulatio illuminat oculos interiores, quia uexatio dat intellectum. Stultus in culpa fit sapiens in pena. Est et collir- [2]

35 2–3 *Que…poposcit*: these verses are also in William de Montibus, *Versarius*, under 'Colliria' (fol. 35r).
5 *Fide purificans corda eorum*: Act 15:9
6 *Qui cadit uidet*: cf. Num 24:16 (Vulg. *uidet qui cadens apertos habet oculos*).
10 *Fel…Thobie*: cf. Tob 11:4–15.
12 *Stultus…pena*: cf. Gratian, D.38 c.10.

35.1 colliriis *subst. for* colliriss *MS* **35.8** hoc *subst. for* hec *MS* **35.12** fit *corr. in MS from* sit

ium diuine preceptionis. Dicitur in psalmo: *Preceptum domini lucidum, illuminans oculos*, scilicet oculos interiores, rationem et intellectum. Alibi dicitur: *Declaratio sermo num tuorum illuminat, et intellectum dat paruulis*. Est et collirium orationis: *Si quis indiget sapientiam, postulet a deo, qui dat omnibus affluenter*. Oratio illuminat intellectum. Vnde Hylarius uolens exponere illud ewangelium, *In principio erat uerbum*, etc., petiit Martinum discipulum suum orare dum exponeret, et ita oratione eius adiutus intellectum habuit magis illuminatum in expositione ewangelii. Est et collirium penitentie. Iesus luto et sputo liniuit oculos ceci, et postea uisum recepit; uere penitens habet oculos linitos luto et sputo quando recognoscit se cinerem et in cinerem reuersurum. Est et collirium operationis bone. Dicitur in psalmo: *A mandatis tuis intellexi*.

Est collirium [3]

F	Fidei,	P	Preceptionis,
V	Humilitatis,	O	Orationis,
I	Ire que est per zelum,	P	Penitentie,
T	Tribulationis,	O	Operat⟨i⟩onis.
		SCIT	

primas: Sillabas

36. De eruditione dei

Qualiter erudiat deus ut tibi notio fiat,
DEM PREBE CONFLA mente tua memora,
Aut hoc commemora bene uerba per hec: BENE COLLA
EXI MINO PREI FLARE DOMAQVE CONI.

13–14 *Preceptum…oculos*[1]: Ps 18:9
15–16 *Declaratio…paruulis*: Ps 118:130
17–18 *Si…affluenter*: Iac 1:5
18–22 *Vnde…ewangelii*: cf. Peter the Chanter, *Verbum adbreuiatum*, textus conflatus 2.34 (CCCM 196:733, lines 24–28); textus alter 89 (CCCM 196b:448, lines 54–56).
19 *In principio erat uerbum*: Io 1:1
22–23 *Iesus…ceci*: cf. Io 9:6
24–25 *recognoscit…reuersurum*: cf. Gen 3:19, Iob 34:15, and above, 17.23–24.
26 *A mandatis tuis intellexi*: Ps 118:104

Deus erudit nos [3]

D	Doctrina quam dat nobis per aliquem magistrum.
E	Exemplo,
M	Miraculo,

Erudit et nos

PRE	Precepto,	CON	Consilio,
BE	Beneficio,	FLA	Flagello.

hoc: Scilicet qualiter erudiat deus. [4]
Deus erudit quandoque

BENE	Beneficii	COLLA	Collat⟨i⟩one.

Deus erudit [5]

EX	Exempli	MI	Miraculi	PRE	Precepti
I	Imitatione,	NO	Nouitate,	I	Instructione,
FLA	Flagelli	DO	Doctrina	CON	Consilii
RE	Restrictione siue district⟨i⟩one,	MAQVE	Magistri,	I	Inspiratione.

37. Hic notatur quibus digne sumi possit sancta eucharistia

Est humili, miti caro sancta, deumque timenti, *101v*
Atque uiatori cibus est ac esurienti.
Huic quoque qui pugnat, sicut pugnans tria uincat.
Quatuor et reges prosternat, quinque prementes.
Melchisedech Abrahe panem uinum quoque digne *102r*
Optulit ut reges superauit quinque prementes.

In psalmo dicitur: *Edent pauperes et saturabuntur*, scilicet pauperes spiritu, scilicet humiles, mundi contemptores, edent sacrificia corporis et san⟨guinis⟩ Cristi sacramentaliter et spiri- [2]

36 16–20 *Deus…Inspiratione*: similarly, *Ex auditis super psalmos*, Ps 2:10 (fol. 9vb): 'Deus erudit nos multipliciter: districtione flagelli, instructione precepti, nouitate miraculi, collatione beneficii, doctrina magistri, imitatione exempli, inspiratione consilii.'

37 6 *Melchisedech…digne*: this verse is adapted above, 2.4.
8 *Edent…saturabuntur*: Ps 21:27

36.13 scilicet *preceded by* q *in MS before corr.* **37.4** uincat *corr. in MS from* uinca*

tualiter. Sacramentaliter edere corpus Cristi est sumere illud sub forma panis et uini. Iudas corpus Cristi tantum sacramentaliter sumpsit, scilicet non spiritualiter. A quibusdam dictum est quod comedit corpus Cristi, quia sacramentaliter sumpsit; a quibusdam dictum est quod non comedit, quia non sumpsit spiritualiter. Spiritualiter sumere corpus Cristi est uniri Cristo et ecclesie. Et sicut in corporali commestione comedens iocundatur, et cibus unitur corpori, et comedens imitatur cibum—scilicet a frigido cibo frigescit, a calido calescit—sic in spirituali sumptione corporis Cristi comedens iocundatur in Cristo—scilicet in bonis operibus—et cibo spirituali unitur, quia corpus Cristi eum sibi incorporat et unit. Et in hoc est differentia huius spiritualis commestionis ad corporalem co⟨mmestionem⟩, quod in hac co⟨mmestione⟩, cibus sumptus incorporat sibi comedentem; et in illa, comedens sibi sumptum cibum incorporat. Imitatur etiam cibum spiritualem sumptum comedens digne corpus Cristi, id est imitatur Cristum in gestis et factis eius, quia sancta eucharistia est cibus humilium; sumentes hunc cibum debent adorare et incuruare se humiliando se in sumptione illius. In psalmo ubi nos habemus: *Edent pauperes et saturabuntur*, hebraica ueritas habet: *Comedent mites et saturabuntur*, scilicet comedent sacrificia corporis et san⟨guinis⟩ Cristi. Sic habetur quod sancta eucharistia cibus est mitium, et ex hoc quod est cibus mitium, colligitur quod rebelles, et inter se discordes, nullo modo debent accedere ad sumptionem eucharistie, sed unanimes et qui sunt *unius moris in domo* possunt accedere. Vnde in Actus apostolorum dicitur: *Erant perdurantes unanimiter in templo, frangentes panem circa domos*, scilicet

12–16 *Iudas... spiritualiter*: cf. Peter Lombard, *Sententiae* 4.11.6.2.

30–31 *Edent... saturabuntur*: Ps 21:27 in the Gallican Psalter, translated from the Septuagint

31 *Comedent... saturabuntur*: Ps 21:27 in Jerome's translation of the Hebrew. This comparison is also made in *Ex auditis super psalmos*, Ps 21:27 (fol. 35rb). Cf. below, 40.88–89 for another instance of comparison between these versions.

36 *unius moris in domo*: Ps 67:7

37–38 *Erant... domos*: Act 2:46

37.28 hunc *corr. in MS from* h** **37.29** se[1] *corr. in MS over eras. by another hand*

panem sanctum, id est corpus Cristi. Dicit Moyses de agno pascali: *Comedetis illum in una domo*. Sic datur intelligi quod unanimes debent esse sumentes uerum agnum paschalem, scilicet Cristum. Catholice concedi potest quod ipse Cristus sumpmitur in sumptione eucharistie, quia ipse ait: *Qui manducat me uiuet propter me*. Est etiam eucharistia cibus timentium deum. Vnde illud: *Escam dedit timentibus se*. Super illum locum dicitur non escam corporalem quam dat etiam non timentibus se, sed escam spiritualem, quia eucaristia est cibus timentium deum; debet sumi cum timore, scilicet cum reuerentia, dei. Corpus Cristi dicitur sanctum in psalmo ubi dicitur: *Nec dabis sanctum tuum uidere corruptionem*. Corpus Cristi requiescens in sepulcro seruabatur illesum et inmune ab omni corruptione, quia deitas unita corpori seruauit corpus ne uermesceret, putresceret, incineraretur. Et dicitur corpus Cristi sanctum, quia portio carnis sumpta de uirgine in sumptione sanctificata est et mundata a fomite peccati. Dicitur etiam sanctum propter effectum, quia amplius sanctificat illum qui sanctus sumit illud.

Sancta eucharistia cibus est uiantium. Vnde Moyses comes- [3]
turis agnum paschalem significantem Cristum dixit: *Habebitis calciamenta in pedibus, tenentes baculos in manibus uestris*. Quasi diceret: Estote preparati et expediti ad sumptionem agni. Viatoris uolentis, ad iter preparare se, est sumere calciamenta in pedibus et baculum in manibus. Ex hoc quod eukaristia est cibus uiantium, innuitur quod hii digne possunt accedere ad sumptionem euka⟨ristie⟩ qui sunt uiatores mundi et ciues celi,

40 *Comedetis…domo*: Ex 12:46
42–43 *sumpmitur = sumitur*
43–44 *Qui…me*: Io 6:58
45 *Escam…se*: Ps 110:5
50 *Nec…corruptionem*: Ps 15:10
55 *fomite*: 'cause,' 'source' (*DMLBS* s.v. *fomes* 4d)
59–60 *Habebitis…uestris*: Ex 12:11

37.40 sic *corr. in MS from* scilicet *by another hand* **37.41** uerum *corr. in MS from* utrum *by another hand* **37.57** sumit *corr. in MS from* summit

qui non habentes hic certam mansionem futuram inquirunt, credentes se esse exules in hac ualle lacrimarum, scilicet in hoc mundo. Est et eucharistia cibus esurientium, unde Iudeis conquerentibus in deserto de fame missum est manna significans corpus Cristi. Ex hoc quod eukaristia est cibus esurientium, intelligitur quod cum deuotione debet sumi, non tali consuetudine quali bos accedit ad presepe ut ex consuetudine proueniat fastidium, quia cibus iste fastidium fastidit, contemptum contempnit. Vnde quidam religiosi non cotidie in septimana conficiunt, ut ex nimia consuetudine proueniens fastidii tollatur occasio, et eis in sumptione eukaristie augeatur deuotio. Dicit Augus⟨tinus⟩: 'Cotidie conficere nec approbo nec uitupero.'

[4] Sancta euka⟨ristia⟩ cibus est pugnantium. Vnde Moyses commesturis agnum pascalem dixit: *Renes uestros accingetis*. Accingi pugnantium est. Ex hoc quod eukaristia cibus est pugnantium, siue potius expugnantium, intelligitur quod hii qui digne uolunt euka⟨ristiam⟩ sumere contra uicia pugnare debent. Et ea expugnate, quia in Apocalipsi dicit dominus: *Vincenti dabo edere de ligno uite*. Lignum uite est ipse Cristus. Et ut digne sumatur euka⟨ristia⟩ pugnandum est contra tria, et expugnanda sunt ea. Pugnandum est contra diabolum, carnem, mundum. Contra diabolum, quia eo expugnato digne sumitur euka⟨ristia⟩. Vnde Pharaone, per quem accipitur diabolus, multis plagis uerberato et iam confuso, populo Israelis in extremis

66 *non... inquirunt*: cf. Hebr 13:14.
67 *in*[1]*... lacrimarum*: this was a popular phrase via Ps 83:7 and the hymn *Salue regina*; the context is similar to Jerome, *Tractatus lix in psalmos*, Ps 136:1 (CCSL 78:295, line 8).
68–69 *Iudeis... manna*: cf. Ex 16.
77 *Cotidie... uitupero*: cf. Augustine, *Epist*. 54.4 (CCSL 31:228–229); Gratian, D.2 c.13; Peter the Chanter, *Verbum adbreuiatum*, textus conflatus 1.21 (CCCM 196:189, lines 177–178); textus prior 23 (CCCM 196a:178, lines 12–13); textus alter 22 (CCCM 196b:124, lines 114–116 and 123–124).
79 *Renes uestros accingetis*: Ex 12:11
83–84 *Vincenti... uite*[1]: Apoc 2:7
88–90 *Pharaone... pascalis*: cf. Ex 12:3–30.

37.66 certam *corr. in MS over eras. by another hand* **37.77** cotidie *corr. in MS from* cotconidie

finibus Egypti, scilicet in Ramesse, comeditur agnus pascalis, significans Cristum. Contra carnem et mundum pugnandum est, quia his expugnatis cum diabolo digne sumitur euka⟨ristia⟩. Vnde Pharaone et Egyptiis submersis, populo Israelis egresso ab Egypto et existenti in deserto Egypto postposita, datum est manna. Sic et uerum manna, scilicet corpus Cristi, digne datur egressis ab Egypto ea postposita, scilicet egressis a mundo contempto et expugnato Pharaone submerso, scilicet diabolo expulso et expugnato, et Egyptiis submersis, scilicet uiciis expulsis et carne expugnata.

tria: Scilicet diabolum, carnem, mundum.

Per ·v· reges accipiuntur ·v· sensus; per ·iiii· reges accipiuntur [5]
·iiii· principalia uicia que sibi subiugant ·v· sensus corporis.

Per hoc quod Melchisedech optulit panem et uinum Abrahe [6–7]
reuertenti a cede ·iiii·or regum qui ·v· reges impugnauerant, datur intelligi quod pugnatores et expugnatores debent esse qui digne sumere uolunt eucharistiam. Et sicut Melchisedech op⟨tulit⟩ pa⟨nem⟩ et ui⟨num⟩ Abra⟨he⟩, reuertenti a cede ·iiii·or regum, sic uerus Melchi⟨sedech⟩, id est Cristus, offeret pa⟨nem⟩ et ui⟨num⟩, scilicet corpus suum et san⟨guinem⟩, reuertenti a cede ·iiii·or regum, scilicet ei qui subiugatione uiciorum a ·v· sensibus excutit.

38. Ex his potest intelligi quid significet candela breuis in medio candelabrum in tribus noctibus ante pascha, et quid per cereum erectum in sabbato pasche

Cristum signantem post candelam breuiorem,
Cereus erigitur, quo Cristus significatur.
Nam surgens magnus, apparuit in cruce paruus.

90 *Ramesse*: cf. Ex 12:37.

93 *Pharaone… submersis*: cf. Ex 14:28.

104 *·v· reges*: i.e. in the story of Melchisedech, Gen 14:17–20 and Hebr 7:1–10 (also used above, 2)

37.91 significans: *superfluous abbreviation in MS* **37.99** carne: *the scribe originally began to write* -ne *in MS in a different location, but moved it and finished the line elsewhere to leave more space for the following gloss* **37.110** uiciorum *corr. in MS from* uciorum

His Cristus tali poterit ratione notari.
Hoc deitas binis unitur, lux ut in illis.

In tribus noctibus tenebrarum ante pascha ponitur parua candela in medio aliarum significans Cristum, et in paschali festo erigitur magnus cereus significans Cristum. **[4–5]**

Per paruam candelam positam in medio aliarum tribus noctibus datur intelligi quod Cristus apparuit paruus in passione. Per magnum cereum datur intelligi quod apparuit magnus in resurrectione. Cristus dicitur ante passionem partim deus, partim homo apparuisse; in passione totus homo; in resurrectione totus deus. Istud idem aliis uerbis dicitur, quia Cristus dicitur ante passionem dormitasse, in passione dormisse, in resurrectione euigilasse. **[6]**

Sicut in candela lux unitur lichno et cere, sic in Cristo unitur deitas anime et corpori. **[7–8]**

hoc: Scilicet Cristo. **[8]**
binis: Anime et corpori.
in illis: Scilicet in candela et cereo, in quibus lux unitur lichno et cere.

39. Hic notantur quedam que sunt necessaria predicatori

Erudiens homines transi, prefulgida nubes
Conspectu domini. Sic ut placeas bonus illi,
Sis leuis atque rigans nubes, sublimis, obumbrans. *102v*
Peniteas opere, fama quoque, dogmate, mente.
Ac incede, prei, procedas: sic bene transi.

38 15–17 *Cristus…deus*: Gilbert de la Porrée, *In Boeth. contra Eut.* 6.5 (ed. Häring, 329); also found in Simon of Tournai, *Expositio in symbolum 'Quicumque'* 7.41 (ed. Häring, 191)
20 *lichno*: 'wick' (*DMLBS* s.v. *lychnus* 2)

39 6 *prei*: the imperative form of *praeeo* is rare.

38.12 paruam *subst. for* unam *MS*, *corr. from* **iam *by another hand*
39.6 incede *corr. in MS from* incende

Sis ignis carbo, grando simul erudiendo;
Velox, pennata, penetrans, directa sagitta, *103r*
Missaque. Nox nocti da scire, diesque diei:
Eructa uerbum. Prudentem te quoque fidum,
Atque super populum domini decet esse statutum, *103v*
Cui des triticeum, mensura, tempore, fructum.

In psalmo dicitur de apostolis: *Prefulgorre in conspectu eius nubes transierunt, grando et carbones ignis*. Potest etiam illud dici de quibuslibet predicatoribus. [2]

Predicator debet transire prefulgida nubes in conspectu domini, scilicet in beneplacito et approbatione dei: non in conspectu diaboli, ut placeat diabolo predicando heresim, faciendo malum; non in conspectu mundi, ut predicet pro questu; non in conspectu hominis, ut predicet pro humano fauore; non in conspectu sui ipsius, ut querat que sua sunt, sed que Iesu Cristi. [3]

Nubes habet leuitatem, irrigationem, altitudinem, obumbrationem. Sic predicator debet esse leuis, scilicet inpiger et strenuus ut Cristus, qui circuibat totam Galileam predicando. Debet etiam habere irrigationem, scilicet instruere alium in fide et bonis moribus; docere ut sit intelligens et requirens deum—intelligens fide, requi⟨rens⟩ opere. Debet etiam habere altitudinem, quia debet eleuari a terra ne inhiet terrenis, sed que sursum sunt sapiat. Debet etiam habere obumbrationem, scilicet obumbrare sed refrigerare mentes fidelium ab estu praue concupiscentie, scilicet ab estu mundialis concupiscentie et ab estu carnalis concupiscentie. [4]

Predicator debet pre aliis lucere officio, dignitate, sapientia, sanctitate, et in multis aliis. Debet habere ful⟨g⟩orem multi- [5]

8 This verse is similar to William de Montibus, *Versarius*, under 'Sagitta' (fol. 107r).

13 *Prefulgorre* = *praefulgorae*, 'very bright' (*DMLBS* s.v. *praefulgorus*); Vulg. *prae fulgore*

13–14 *Prefulgorre…ignis*: Ps 17:13

39.13 eius *written twice in MS before corr.* **39.27** habere *corr. in MS from* h** *by another hand* **39.29** habere *corr. in MS from* h*** *by another hand*

plicem. Debet enim habere fulgorem operationis bone. Vnde illud: *Luceant opera uestra coram hominibus, ut glorificent patrem uestrum qui est in celis*. Bene dicitur, ‘ut glo⟨rificent⟩ pa⟨trem⟩,’ quia eo fine debent opera lucere, ‘ut glo⟨rificent⟩ pa⟨trem⟩ qui est in celis,’ non ut per opera fauor aut humana gratia requiratur. Debet etiam habere fulgorem opinionis bone, scilicet sinceritatem fame. Qui uult esse uere Cristianus habeat suauitatem serenate conscientie et sinceritatem fame. Et sic erit unctus uero crismate. Crisma conficitur ex oleo et balsamo. Per oleum accipitur suauitas sere⟨nate⟩ conscientie; per bal⟨samum⟩, quod est odoriferum, accipitur since⟨ritatem⟩ fame, que est necessaria homini propter proximum. Debet etiam predi⟨cator⟩ habere fulgorem doctrine, scilicet theologice doctrine et theologice scientie, quia dicitur: *Preceptum domini lucidum, illuminans oculos*. Et dicit Salomon: *Mandatum lucerna est; lex, lux*. Debet etiam predicator habere oleum in uase, sicut uirgo prudens, scilicet nitorem glorie in uase bone conscientie. Dicit Paulus: *Gloria nostra hec est, testimonium conscientie nostre*.

[6] Est transitus incedendo, precedendo, procedendo; est etiam tandem transitus dece⟨de⟩ndo. Qualiter predicatores debeant incedere, haberi potest a Moyse ita dicente Leuitis: *Transite a porta ad portam per medium castrorum et occidat unusquisque*, etc. Sic predi⟨catores⟩ transire debent per me⟨dium⟩ cas⟨trorum⟩, scilicet recte incedere a uicia ad uicium increpando

36–37 *Luceant…celis*: a common abbreviation of Mt 5:16, notably found in Peter Lombard, *Commentarium in Psalmos*, Ps 25:8 (PL 191:265a)
41–46 *Qui…proximum*: discussed in more detail above, 26.5–11
48–49 *Preceptum…oculos*: Ps 18:9
49–50 *Mandatum…lux*: Prov 6:23
50–51 *oleum…prudens*: cf. Mt 25:1–13.
52–53 *Gloria…nostre*: 2 Cor 1:12
56–58 *Transite…unusquisque*: Ex 32:27. For the substitution of *transite* for Vulg. *redite*, cf. Peter Lombard, *Commentarium in Psalmos*, Ps 73:15 (PL 191:689c).

39.41 fame: bone *add. MS before corr.* **39.43** erit *corr. in MS from* tem **39.46** que *corr. in MS from* quia *by another hand* **39.49** salomon *subst. for* salomonon *MS*

et nemini parcere, sicut Leuite, pro nullo flexi, nec fratribus nec cognatis parcebant. Debent etiam precedere, secundum quod dicit Iosue: *Ite ante fratres uestros omnes armati et manufortes et pugnate pro eis*. Debent etiam procedere, scilicet ad perfectionem, secundum hoc quod a domino dicitur Abrahe: *Ambula coram me et esto perfectus*. Transibunt tandem predi⟨catores⟩ decedendo de mundo ad patrem. De hoc transitu dicit Daniel: *Pertransibunt plurimi et multiplex erit scientia*. Decedentibus dottoribus noui superuenient. Et hoc fuit quod *aliis et aliis uasis ferebantur* cibi in conuiuio Assueri. Et hoc fuit quod in sabbato panibus propositionis in mensa supponebantur alii panes triticei, noui, calidi. Doctores in sacra scriptura debent hoc attendere, scilicet quod triticei pa⟨nes⟩ et no⟨ui⟩ et ca⟨lidi⟩ superpo⟨nebantur⟩ in mensa, quia ipsi debent esse triticei (habere contritionem cordis), noui (habendo uite nouitatem), calidi (caritate feruentes).

[7] Carbo igne accensus dat splendorem et calorem; sic predicatores dare debent aliis splen⟨dorem⟩ et ca⟨lorem⟩. Debent facere alios habere cognitionem dei et feruorem karitatis. Grando dura ferit cum sonitu; feriens mollia cito mollescit. Sic predicatores superbos et rebelles ferire debent dura increpatione et minis, et humiles mulcere blandiciis. De predicatoribus dicitur: *Virtutem terribilium tuorum dicent, et magnitudinem tuam narrabunt. Memoriam habundantie suauitatis tue eructabunt, et iusticia tua exultabunt*. Debent itaque predicatores prius in-

62–63 *Ite* ... *eis*: Ios 1:14
62 *manufortes* = *fortes manu* in Vulg. (*DMLBS* s.v. *manufortis*)
64–65 *Ambula*... *perfectus*: Gen 17:1
67 *Pertransibunt*... *scientia*: Dan 12:4
68 *dottoribus* = *doctoribus*
68–69 *aliis*[1]... *ferebantur*: Esth 1:7
69–71 *in*[2]... *calidi*: cf. 1 Sam 21:6, Lev 24:5–9.
82–84 *Virtutem*... *exultabunt*: Ps 144:6–7

39.66 transitu dicit *corr. in MS from* transitudine **39.68** et aliis *om. MS before corr.; add. above the line by another hand* **39.70** alii *corr. in MS from* elii *by another hand* | triticei *corr. in MS from* tritici **39.72** et[1] *om. MS before corr.; add. above the line* **39.73** triticei: sed *add. MS before corr.* **39.79** cito mollescit *corr. in MS from* citemollescit **39.82** dicent... tuam *corr. in MS over eras. by another hand*

crepare et postea demulcere. Moyses etiam, qui mansuetissimus erat, faciebat increpationes, dicens: *Generatio praua et peruersa! Hecine reddis deo, popule stulte et inspiens?* Et Iohannes increpauit, dicens: *Genimina uiperarum*, etc. Et Paulus dixit: *O insensati Galate!*, etc.

[8] Sagitta habet uelocitatem, pennas quibus bene uolet, uim penetratiuam, directionem. Sic predicator debet habere uelocitatem. Dictum est predicatoribus: *Neminem in uia salutaueritis.* Et sic intelligitur quod festinandum est eis, quia opus est. Debet etiam habere pennas uirtutum quibus bene uolet. Debet etiam habere uim penetratiuam, scilicet uiua uoce doctrine penetrare corda auditorum, secundum quod dicitur: *Viuus est dei sermo et efficax et penetrabilior omni gladio ancipite.* Debet etiam habere directionem et uolare per medium celi, sicut in Apocalipsi legitur aquila uolare per medium celi, per quem significatur predicator, qui debet habere directionem, et non flecti nimis, uel prece uel premio.

[9] In psalmo dicitur: *Misit sagittas suas*, scilicet predicatores. Per hoc quod dicitur, 'misit,' intelligitur quod non debet quis predicare nisi mittatur. Dicit Cristus de pseudoprophetis: *Currebant et ego non mittebam eos.* Est exterior missio et est interior. Exterior est quando aliquis ordinatur in diaconum siue sacer-

86–87 *Generatio…inspiens*: Deut 32:5–6
88 *Genimina uiperarum*: Lc 3:7
89 *O…Galate*: Gal 3:1
92 *Neminem…salutaueritis*: Lc 10:4; for the variant *in*, cf. Augustine, sermon 101 (ed. Lambot, 51, lines 29–30)
96–97 *Viuus…ancipite*: Hebr 4:12
99 *aquila…celi*: cf. Apoc 8:13.
102 *Misit…suas*: Ps 17:15
104 *de pseudoprophetis*: Samuel Presbiter also wrote a poem entitled *De pseudoprophetis* in *Ad habendam memoriam*, fols 184v–187v.
104–105 *Currebant…eos*: Ier 23:21 (Vulg. *non mittebam prophetas et ipsi currebant*)

39.89 etc *om. MS before corr.; add. by another hand* **39.92** salutaueritis *corr. in MS from* salutauitis *by another hand* **39.99** uolare *corr. in MS from* uo** *by another hand* **39.101** prece *corr. in MS from* prerce **39.103–104** predicare *corr. in MS from* pdicare **39.105** exterior *corr. in MS from* exertior

dotem, quia ex hoc quod accepit talem ordinem et ex debito officii iam missus est ad predicandum. Est etiam exterior missio quando pontifex iubet aliquem predicare, quia ex precipientis auctoritate et obedientie necessitate iam missus est ad predicandum. Interior missio est que fit familiari consilio et inspiratione spiritus sancti. In psalmo dicitur de apostolis: *Dies diei eructat uerbum, et nox nocti indicat scientiam.* Per hoc intelligitur quod predicator debet discrete predicare. Debet esse 'dies diei,' scilicet clarus claro, spiritualis spirituali. 'Dies' dicitur a 'dian' Greco, quod est 'claritas' Latine. Et per hoc quod dicitur, 'dies diei,' notatur quod predicator debet esse primo clarus uita et fama, et postea aliis predicare. Per hoc quod dicitur, 'eructa⟨t⟩,' notatur quod predi⟨cator⟩ debet habere primo plenitudinem sapientie et postea predicare. Ioseph primo impleuit horrea et postea distribuit; Dauid sapientissimus sedit in cathedra doctrinali. Et dictum est: *Cum Ecclesiastes factus erat sapientissimus, edocuit populum.* Debet etiam predicator esse nox nocti. Debet celare alta misteria, et fieri minor minori et rudi condescendendo ei. Et debet indicare ei scientiam, scilicet fidem humanitatis Cristi, uel indicare scientiam, scilicet fidem et bonos mores, docendo qualiter conuersandum sit *in medio huius nationis praue et peruerse.* Potest etiam notari quod debeat esse discretio in predicatione per hoc quod dicit Paulus quibusdam rudibus: *Nihil arbitratus sum me scire inter uos*

112–113 *Dies…scientiam*: Ps 18:3; most of the following material is also found in the commentary on this verse in *Ex auditis super psalmos* (fols 38vb–39ra), which takes the psalm as describing the preaching of the apostles.

116 *dian* ≈ δῖος (neuter δῖον), 'bright' or 'shining' in Homeric usage; cf. William of Conches, *Glosae super Platonem* 1.95 (CCCM 203:169, lines 28–29).

120–121 *Ioseph…distribuit*: cf. Gen 41:49, 41:56.

121–122 *Dauid…doctrinali*: cf. 2 Sam 23:8.

122–123 *Cum…populum*: Eccl 12:9

124–125 *fieri…rudi*: cf. 1 Cor 9:19–22.

127–128 *in…peruerse*: Phil 2:15

130–131 *Nihil…crucifixum*: 1 Cor 2:2

39.114 esse *corr. in MS from* eruc⟨tare⟩ *by another hand* **39.116** claritas *corr. in MS from* cantas **39.123** esse: *lacuna in MS before corr.; add. in another hand*

nisi Iesum Cristum et hunc crucifixum. Lac uobis potum dedi, non escam. Dicit etiam: *Inter sapientes loquor sapientiam. Omnibus omnia facta sumus. Siue mente excedimus deo, siue sobrii sumus uobis.* Sic datur intelligi quod predicatores clari claris, spirituales spiritualibus, sapientes sapientibus, maiores maioribus fieri debent predicando eis maiora. Minoribus uero debent condescendere, et minora predicare.

Quod habenda sit discretio in predicatione notatur per quedam [10]
uasa, scilicet phialas et ciathos que in ueteri testamento erant posita in templo ad suscipiendum libamenta: arida ut sal, thus, et huiusmodi; liquida ut uinum, oleum, et huiusmodi. Phiala erat uas habens latum os, strictum fundum, per quod significatur quod predicator sapientibus et capacibus doctrine plene debet effundere uerba doctrine que habet in corde. Ciathus erat uas habens strictum os et latum fundum, per quod significatur quod predi⟨cator⟩ minoribus et rudibus pauca debet fundere, et multa corde reseruare cum ipsi non sint capaces doctrine.

eructa uerbum: Scilicet illud uerbum quod *erat in principio apud deum*, id est, Predica diuinitatem Cristi.

131–132 *Lac…escam*: 1 Cor 3:2

132 *Inter…sapientiam*: 1 Cor 2:6 (Vulg. *sapientiam autem loquimur inter perfectos*)

132–133 *Omnibus…sumus*: 1 Cor 9:22

133–134 *Siue…uobis*: 2 Cor 5:13

139–140 *phialas…libamenta*: cf. Ex 25:29, 37:16; Peter Lombard, *Commentarium in Psalmos*, Ps 18:2 (PL 191:207d–208a).

139 *ciathos = cyathos*

140–141 *arida…huiusmodi*[2]: cf. Lev 2.

141–148 *Phiala…doctrine*: cf. Gregory the Great, *Moralia in Iob* 20.2.4 (CCSL 143a:1004, lines 37–44); Peter the Chanter, *Verbum adbreuiatum*, textus conflatus 1.63 (CCCM 196:427, lines 88–98); textus alter 50 (CCCM 196b:260, lines 53–60).

149–150 *erat…deum*: Io 1:2

39.138 quod *corr. in MS from* quantum *by another hand* | per *corr. in MS over eras. by another hand* **39.140** suscipiendum *subst. for* suspiciendum *MS* | arida *corr. in MS from* auida *by another hand* **39.141** uinum *corr. in MS from* tucium **39.150** diuinitatem *corr. in MS from* diuinatem

Notari potest discretionem esse habendam in predicatione per [10–11] hoc quod dicitur in ewangelio: *Quis, putas, est fidelis seruus et prudens quem constituit dominus super familiam suam ut det illis in tempore tritici mensuram?* Predicator siue prelatus in ecclesia debet esse fidelis et prudens. Pauci sunt fideles, pauciores sunt prudentes; ·iiii·^{or} attendenda sunt circa fidelitatem predi⟨catoris⟩ siue prela⟨ti⟩. Debet esse fidelis predicando ut nihil adulterinum, nihil adulterina adiuratione corruptum predicet; scilicet non errores siue hereses predicet, non falsum sed uerum predicet. Per hoc quod dicitur, 'quem constituit dominus,' notatur quod debet esse fidelis introeundo, scilicet intrare per ostium, id est per Cristum. Et ostiarius debet eum introducere, scilicet spiritus sanctus, et non Symon Magus, scilicet symonia—non fauor humanus, non iussus regius siue timor regius, uel aliquid huiusmodi. Per hoc quod dicitur, 'det,' duo attenduntur, scilicet quod non debet uendere pro nummo fauoris, uel uendere pro nummo pecunie, quia dicitur: *Gratis accepistis, gratis date*. Predicator debet laxare retia in capturam animarum, non in capturam pecuniarum. Fidelis dispensator non commodum suum siue fauorem humanum attendit, sed commodum domini sui. Circa prudentiam predi⟨catoris⟩ ·iiii·^{or} attenduntur que notantur per hoc quod dicitur: 'illis in tempore tritici mensuram.' Per hoc quod dicitur, 'illis,' scilicet famulis dei, notatur quod predicare debet dignis, non indignis, scilicet non canibus siue porcis—canibus, scilicet oblatrantibus et

152–154 *Quis…mensuram*: a conflation of Mt 24:45 and Lc 12:42 (also used below, 42.16–18)

155–156 *Pauci…prudentes*: Peter Lombard, *Commentarium in Psalmos*, Ps 18:2 (PL 191:207c)

161–162 *fidelis…introducere*: cf. Io 10:2–9.

162–163 *Et…symonia*: see also Samuel's more pointed attack against corrupt church officials in his paraphrase of Psalm 1 as discussed in Dinkova-Bruun, 'Samuel Presbyter and the Glosses to his Versification of Psalm 1.'

163 *Symon Magus*: cf. Act 8:18–20.

167 *Gratis…date*: Mt 10:8

39.158 adiuratione *corr. in MS from* aniutione **39.161** intrare *corr. in MS from* intro **39.165** quod: *the scribe began to write* hoc *in MS before corr.*

obtrectantibus; porcis, scilicet conculcantibus et fastidientibus uerbum dei. Per hoc quod dicitur, 'in tempore,' notatur quod obseruandum est tempus predicandi, quia est *tempus tacendi et tempus loquendi. Omnia tempus habent.* Predicator debet obseruare quando auiditatem audiendi habent auditores. Per hoc quod dicitur, 'tritici,' notatur quod predi⟨cator⟩ illa que magis edificant debet predicare, et quisquilias et paleas, scilicet illa que minus edificant, omittere; triticum, scilicet frumentum, dare debet predicator pocius quam ordeum. Ordeum uidetur dare Paulus, ubi dicit: *Vidua, si soluta est a uiro, nubat si uelit.* Frumentum dat, dicens: *Beatior erit, si sic permanserit.* Per hoc quod dicitur, 'mensuram,' notatur quod modum in predicatione debet obseruare predi⟨cator⟩, quia imponit finem sapiens et rebus honestis:

Est modus in rebus, sunt certi denique fines
Quos ultra citraque nequit ⟨con⟩sistere rectum.

Predicatio, si nimis est assidua, uilescit. Si rara, non sufficit.

40. De bono circuitu faciendo

Scripta, creaturas, exemplaque, premia, penas, *104r*
Dona dei, mentem, peccata, fidemque per orbem
Auctam circueas. Loca, tempora, menbra reuoluas

177–178 *tempus*[2]*...loquendi*: Eccl 3:7
178 *Omnia tempus habent*: Eccl 3:1; also used below, 42.15–16
184 *Vidua...uelit*: Rom 7:2–3, 1 Cor 7:39; these are paired similarly above, 18.7–8.
185 *Beatior...permanserit*: 1 Cor 7:40
189–190 *Est...rectum*: Horace, *Sermones* 1.1.106–107; cf. Peter the Chanter, *Verbum adbreuiatum*, textus conflatus 2.27 (CCCM 196:707, lines 72–73); textus alter 83 (CCCM 196b:431, lines 49–50).
191 *Predicatio...sufficit*: also used below, 42.14–15; cf. Peter Lombard, *Collectanea in omnes Pauli apostoli Epistulas*, Hebr 6:4 (PL 192:444a) and Peter the Chanter, *Verbum adbreuiatum*, textus conflatus 1.32 (CCCM 196:240, line 92), 1.54 (367, line 176). Later cited by Thomas of Chobham, *Summa de commendatione et extirpatione uirtutum* 4 (CCCM 82b:182, lines 2683–2685).

39.176 obtrectantibus *subst. for* obtractantibus *MS* **39.182** frumentum *subst. for* sfrumentum *MS* **39.190** rectum *subst. for* tectum *MS*

Et circumstantes tua res peccata grauantes.
Post hos circuitus, bene fit cantatio, psalmus.

[2] In psalmo dicitur: *Circuiui, et immolaui in tabernaculo eius hostiam uociferationis; cantabo, et psalmum dicam domino.* Diuersos circuitus debet facere fidelis: debet enim circuire scripta et diuersas auctoritates in sacra scriptura, et in scriptis considerare que sint precepta et que consilia, et que prohi⟨bi⟩tiones et que permissiones, et que sint in scriptis promissa, et que cerimonialia et que moralia; et de moralibus que sint temporalia (sicut quedam que obseruanda sunt in uno tempore, et in alio non), et que sint localia (sicut quedam que obseruanda sunt quibusdam personis, et aliis non), et que sint condicionalia (sicut quedam que fiunt sub conditione, uel manifesta uel latenti). Debet etiam considerare que sint mera et absoluta licet non sint perpetua (sicut mandata de fide), et que sint mera et absoluta et perpetua (sicut illud mandatum: *Diliges dominum deum tuum ex toto corde tuo*, etc.). Debet etiam considerare que precepta in sacra scriptura sint temptationis et probationis, sicut erat illud preceptum quod fecit deus Abrahe quando iussit ut immolaret filium suum. Debet etiam consi⟨derare⟩ precepta que fiunt causa meditationis, ut illud preceptum: *Diliges dominum deum tuum ex toto corde tuo*, etc. Hoc preceptum non potest impleri in uia, sed ideo precipitur ut meditemur qualiter deus sit diligendus, et ut impleatur in patria. Debet consi⟨derare⟩ que precepta fiant causa uitandi fauoris, sicut illud preceptum quod fecit dominus leproso quando iussit ne cui indicaret se mundatum. Debet etiam consi⟨derare⟩ que precepta fiant causa impletionis, sicut illud:

40 6 *cantatio psalmus*: both to be taken with *fit* (i.e. through zeugma)
7–8 *Circuiui…domino*: Ps 26:6. Most of the commentary in this section also found in *Ex auditis super psalmos*, Ps 26:6 (fols 40vb–41ra).
21 *Diliges…tuo*: Deut 6:5; Mt 22:37; Mc 12:30; Lc 10:27
30–31 *dominus…mundatum*: cf. Mt 8:4; Mc 1:44.

40.7 in[1]: *preceding this, the scribe repeated* predicatio…sufficit *from the previous passage before crossing it out* **40.11** considerare *subst. for* considerate *MS* **40.14** obseruanda *corr. in MS from* obseruandi *by another hand* **40.32** fiant *corr. in MS from* fiunt

Honora patrem tuum et matrem tuam, et multa alia mandata que possunt impleri in uia. Debet etiam fidelis circuire diuersas creaturas que singule pariunt materiam laudis diuine. Totus mundus liber est sapientis; cathalogus creaturarum theatrum est psallentium. Debet etiam fidelis circuire exempla bonorum ad imitandum: debet enim attendere iusticiam Abel, pacientiam Iob, fidem Abrahe, mansuetudinem Moysi, et ita aliorum bonos mores debet attendere, et in eis eos imitari. Debet etiam circuire exempla prauorum ad deuitandum. Debet etiam fidelis circuire premia bonorum et attendere quod quidam habent fructum tricesimum, quidam sexagesimum, quidam centesimum; et quod quidam habent auream tantum, quidam auream et auriolam, sicut predicatores, mundi contemptores, martyres, uirgines. Hec sunt ·iiii·$^{o\langle r\rangle}$ priuilegiata: predicatio, mundi contemptus, martyrium, uirginitas. Et debet attendere quod *diuerse sunt mansiones in domo patris*, que intus se differunt sicut stella a stella differt in claritate. Debet etiam fidelis circuire penas malorum et attendere quod plurime sunt pene in inferno et differentes, quia sicut stella a stella differt in claritate, ita umbra ab umbra differt in obscuritate. Debet etiam attendere penas malorum quas habent in presenti uita—sicut penam Herodis et penam Nabugodonosor qui ·vii· annis uixit ut bestia—et ita per con-

33 *Honora... tuam*: Ex 20:12; Mc 7:10

35–36 *Totus... sapientis*: the first line of a sermon given by William de Montibus (extract in Goering, *William de Montibus*, 530, no. 15) and of a brief *Tractatus de homine et membris eius* (noted in Hunt, 'The Collections of a Monk of Bardney,' 28)

36 *cathalogus creaturarum*: Peter Comestor, *Scolastica Historia: Liber Genesis* 2 (CCCM 191:9, line 10), uses this phrase with reference to the *Benedicite* (Dan 3:57–88), sung at Lauds on Sundays and feasts (cited below, lines 114–115).

44 *auriolam = aureolam*

47–49 *Et... claritate*: Peter Lombard, *Collectanea in omnes Pauli apostoli Epistulas*, Eph 1:15 (PL 192:177b)

47–48 *diuerse... patris*: Io 14:2

53 *penam Herodis*: cf. Act 12:23; below, 48.28–29.

54 *Nabugodonosor... bestia*: cf. Dan 4:28–30.

40.33 patrem tuum *corr. in MS from* patre **40.36** cathalogus... theatrum *subst. for* carhalogus... theartum *MS* **40.43** quidam centesimum *corr. in MS from* quida centenum **40.47–49** debet... claritate *om. MS before corr. through homoeoteleuton; add. in marg. in same hand but darker ink* **40.48** intus *corr. in MS from* inter **40.52** malorum *corr. in MS from* mal**

siderationem pene alterius sibi cauere potest. Vnde dicitur de iusto: *Manus suas lauabit in sanguine peccatoris*, id est mundabit se et cauebit sibi per penam peccatoris.
exempla: Bonorum ad imitandum. Malorum ad deuitandum.
premia: Bonorum.
penas: Malorum.

[3] Debet etiam fidelis circuire dona dei et beneficia, et attendere quod deus contulerit naturalia bona (rationem, ingenium, memoriam, et huiusmodi) et dona gratuita (fidem, spem, caritatem, et huiusmodi). Debet etiam fidelis circuire mentem a simili boni militis qui uallo et fossatis munit castrum, ne hosti pateat aditus. Debet etiam fidelis circuire peccata, ut de his conteratur, et ea confiteatur, et de eis satisfaciat. Et debet fidelis circuire numerum recte credentium auctum, ut ex hoc deum laudet et magnificet.

[4] In circumeundo peccata debet fidelis circuire et memorando reuoluere loca, tempora, menbra. Loca, quia debet attendere quid commiserit in uno loco, quid in alio. Debet etiam circuire loca in itinere peregrinationis, sicut loca sepulcri Cristi et alia loca, ubi requiescunt reliquie sanctorum. Debet circumire tempora, quia debet attendere quid commiserit in uno tempore, quid ⟨in⟩ alio: quid in iuuentute, quid in uirili etate, quid in senectute. In psalmo dicitur: *Cogitabo pro peccato meo*. Et alibi dicitur: *Recogitabo tibi omnes annos meos in amaritudine anime mee*. Debet circumire menbra, quia debet attendere que commiserit per ·v· sensus corporeos.

[5] Debet etiam fidelis circumire et memorando reuoluere circumstantias aggrauantes peccata. Debet enim attendere si in sacro loco fecerit turpitudinem, si in tempore abstinentie quando esset ieiunandum fecerit quod non debuit facere, et si ipse in

56 *Manus…peccatoris*: Ps 57:11

64–66 *Debet…aditus*: cf. below, 50.27–28, and Peter the Chanter, *Verbum adbreuiatum*, textus conflatus 1.87 (CCCM 196:601, lines 68–71); textus alter 68 (CCCM 196b:372, lines 62–65).

77 *Cogitabo…meo*: Ps 37:19

78 *Recogitabo…mee*: Is 38:15

40.58 deuitandum *corr. in MS from* deuitadum **40.64** circuire *corr. in MS from* circuirei

peccatis quesunt et appetierunt occasiones peccandi, et alias huiusmodi circumstantes debet circuire.

Ex hoc quod fidelis circuit ea que predicuntur, dat deo sacrificium laudis, et bene operari nititur. Vbi nos habemus *hostiam uociferationis*, hebraica ueritas habet *hostias iubili*. Iubilus est uox innuitiua gaudii quod nec omnino taceri potest pre dulcedine, nec omnino exprimi pro rei laudate magnitudine. Et pro laudantis infirmitate per cantationem datur intelligi interior iocunditas, quia cantus exprimit leticiam mentis. Vnde poeta dicit: [6]

Cantus, animi felicia leti
Argumenta, sonant.

Per psalmum datur intelligi bona operatio que debet sequi cantationem. Psalmus dicebatur modulatio que fiebat ante archam federis domini cum psalterio. Et hec nomen 'psalmus' transumitur ad appellandum 'tractatus,' qui modulabantur cum psalterio. Psalterium resonat tactu manuum, in quo designatur operatio, et reddit sonum a superiori, in quo designatur superna merces. Et ita per psalmum datur intelligi operatio pro superna mercede, scilicet bona operatio. Debent autem alternari hic duo: cantatio et bona operatio. Vnde Esdras in quibusdam titulis psalmorum posuit 'canticum psalmi,' in quibus-

87–88 *sacrificium laudis*: cf. Ps 106:22.
88–89 *hostiam uociferationis*: Ps 26:6 in the Gallican psalter
89 *hostias iubili*: Ps 26:6 in Jerome's translation of the Hebrew; another comparison between these versions above, 37.30–31
Iubilus = *iubilum*
90 *innuitiua*: 'suggestive of,' 'hinting at'
95–96 *Cantus…sonant*: Ovid, *Metamorphoses* 4.761–762
98–103 *Psalmus…merces*: also found in *Ex auditis super psalmos*, Ps 2:1 (fol. 9rb)
100 *tractatus*: i.e. the tract (normally *tractus*), sung in place of the Alleluia at certain penitential Masses (*DMLBS* s.v. *tractatus* 6)
105–107 *Vnde…cantici*: cf. Peter Lombard, *Commentarium in Psalmos*, Ps. 4.intro (PL 191:83a).
106 *canticum psalmi*: found in the titles to Pss. 47, 65, 82, 87, and 107

40.87 dat *corr. in MS from* date **40.89** iubili *subst. for* iubilationis *MS* **40.97** psalmum *subst. for* spalmum *MS* **40.98** modulatio *corr. in MS from* modudoli*catu*

dam 'psalmus cantici.' Sed nusquam posuit 'psalmus psalmi,' nec 'canticum cantici.' Et ita ostensum est quod alternatio facienda est inter cantationem et operationem, et nec semper cantandum est, nec semper operandum, quia quiescenti agendum est, et agenti quiescendum est. Et hoc innuitur in matutinis cum, post diutinum laborem, quasi ludendo discurritur per diuersas creaturas laudando deum in illo cantico quod dicitur: *Benedicite omnia opera domini domino*, etc.

41. In his notatur quod quatuor de causis deus differat dare conuersis ad se sanitatem

Sepe deus multis differt dare dona salutis: *104v*
Vt contemplentur in que mala precipitentur,
Ac attendentes sint amplius illa cauentes,
Et ne sic iustos, ut statim liberet ipsos,
Se credant fieri, det et horum pena uideri
Quod non conuersi magis his sint excruciandi.

Quatuor sunt cause quare deus differat dare sanitatem conuer- **[3–8]**
sis ad se: ut attendat homo in que mala se precipitauerit; et ut caueat sibi amplius, considerans difficultatem in sanitate recoperanda; et ne putet se ad tantam perfectionem uenisse, ut statim audiat ipso orante: *Ecce assum, quia uocasti me;* et ut ostendatur quanta pena sit debita non conuersis, cum tanta difficultate restauretur conuersus.

107 *psalmus cantici*: found at Pss. 29, 66, 67, 74, 86, and 91
114 *Benedicite…domino*: Dan 3:57 (see above, line 36.)

41 3–8 These verses also appear (in a slightly inferior form) in London, Lambeth Palace Library, MS Sion L40.2/L12, fol. 8r, a thirteenth- or fourteenth-century miscellany written in Dover.
11–12 *recoperanda* = *recuperanda*
13 *Ecce…me*: 1 Sam 3:6, 3:9. For *ecce assum*, cf. Gen 46:2; Num 22:38; Is 52:6, 58:9.

40.113 per *corr. in MS from* p **41.1** quatuor *subst. for* sex *MS* (*copied from the following section*) **41.8** excruciandi *corr. in MS from* excirutiandi **41.11** considerans *subst. for* consideratis *MS*

42. Hic notatur quod sex de causis pleraque solent taceri

Quosdam sex cause quedam fecere tacere.

[2] Quandoque tacentur aliqua pro auditorum indignitate, pro auditorum infirmitate, pro scandalo uitando, pro fastidio tollendo, propter reseruationem, propter maioris mali uitationem. Pro audi⟨torum⟩ indig⟨nitate⟩, quia ut dicit Ieronimus, septuaginta interpretes subticuerunt archana trinitatis incarnationis gentibus quas indignas reputabant ad hec recipienda. Pro au⟨ditorum⟩ infir⟨mitate⟩, quia dominus discipulis dixit: *Multa habeo uobis dicere que non potestis portare modo*. Pro scan⟨dalo⟩ uitando, unde dominus post transfigurationem precepit discipulis ne cui dicerent uisionem, ne gentes postea scandalizarentur in cruce eius. Pro fas⟨tidio⟩ tol⟨lendo⟩, quia prudens predicator cauet ne ingerat fastidium nimis assidua predicatione. Predicatio, si fuerit assidua, uilescit; si rara, non sufficit. *Omnia tempus habent*. Dicitur in ewangelio: *Quis putas est fidelis seruus et prudens quem constituit dominus super familiam suam ut det illis in tempore tritici mensuram?* Propter reser⟨uationem⟩, quia Moyses multa reseruauit prophetis, p⟨ro⟩phete Cristo, Cristus apostolis. Vnde Paulus multa instituit in ecclesia que non erant instituta ante passionem Cristi, et ita alii apostoli. Prophete etiam reseruauerunt angelo nomen Cristi, scilicet hoc nomen 'Iesus.' Propter maioris mali uitationem, quia Cristus Sydoniis et Tyris subticuit uerbum predicationis, ne ipsi ex contemptu uerbi fierent deteriores.

42 6–7 *Ieronimus...gentibus*: the same opinion is found in Peter Abelard, *Theologia christiana* 2.15 (CCCM 12:140, lines 253–256), though he does not ascribe it to Jerome, who in fact argues the opposite in *Epistulae* 106.44 (CSEL 55:268, line 6).

7 *subticuerunt*: 'leave unspoken,' 'suppress' (*DMLBS* s.v. *subticere* 2)

9–10 *Multa...modo*: Io 16:12

11–12 *dominus...uisionem*: cf. Mt 17:9, Mc 9:8.

14–15 *Predicatio...sufficit*: cf. above, 39.192.

15–16 *Omnia...habent*: Eccl 3:1; also used above, 39.179

16–18 *Quis...mensuram*: a conflation of Mt 24:45 and Lc 12:42; also used above, 39.152–154

22–23 *angelo...Iesus*: cf. Mt 1:21, Lc 1:31.

23–24 *Sydoniis et Tyris*: cf. Mt 11:21–22, 15:21; Mc 3:8.

43. De sollicitudine

Prouida nature, pastoralis quoque cure
Sollicitudo ualet, et que fit uti bona seruet.
Que fit peccato, prohibetur sollicitudo. *105r*

Prouida sollicitudo nature licita est et bona, quia homo de- [2]
bet prouidere sibi in necessariis, quod potest uideri ex hoc quod Cristus loculos habuit quos commisit inde deteriori in consortio suo, in quo datur intelligi quod nescienti uacare contemplationi, commitenda est administratio temporalium, ut alii, scientes uacare contemplationi, non impediantur interiectione tem poralium. Bona est quoque sollicitudo pastoris quam habet circa instructionem proximorum. De hac dicit Paulus: *Qui preest in sollicitudine*. Et alibi dicit: *Preter hec que extrinsecus sunt, instantia mea cothidiana, et sollicitudo omnium ecclesiarum.*

Sollicitudo que fit ad conseruationem fidei, spei, caritatis, et [3]
aliarum uirtutum bona est. Vnde dicitur: *Solliciti seruare unitatem spiritus in uinculo pacis.*

Sollicitudo que est circa mala facienda mala est. Solli⟨citudo⟩ [4]
etiam immoderata circa necessaria mala est et prohibetur in ewangelio, ubi dicitur: *Ne solliciti sitis anime uestre quid manducetis, aut corpori uestro quid induamini*. Et Paulus dicit: *Nihil solliciti sitis, sed in omni expectatione petitiones uestre innotescant apud deum.*

43 5 *Prouida sollicitudo*: this concept is found in Cassiodorus and Gregory the Great; it is perhaps taken here from *Moralia in Iob* 32.21.41 (CCSL 143b:1659, line 39).

7 *Cristus…deteriori*: cf. Io 12:6.

12–13 *Qui…sollicitudine*: Rom 12:8

13–15 *Preter…ecclesiarum*: 2 Cor 11:28

14 *cothidiana = cotidiana*

17–18 *Solliciti…pacis*: Eph 4:3

21–22 *Ne…induamini*: Mt 6:25 (*aut* is an attested variant for Vulg. *neque*.)

23–24 *Nihil…deum*: Phil 4:6 (abbreviated)

43.7 cristus *subst. for* cristo *MS*

44. De permissione et accusatione

Est permissio triplex, accusatio triplex;
Tu distinguendo CIS atque DIV memorato.

Est permissio ⟨Est accusatio⟩ **[3]**
C Confessionis, D Denunciantis,
I Indulgentie, I Infamantis,
S Sustinentie. V Vlciscentis.

Accusatio denunciantis precipitur. Accu⟨satio⟩ infa⟨mantis⟩ prohibetur. Accusa⟨tio⟩ ul⟨ciscentis⟩ permittitur.

45. In his habetur que portam uite latam et que artam efficiant

Ingresso portam uite faciunt tria latam:
Consuetudo boni, bona spes, dilectio Cristi.
Si iocunderis terrenis, tuque frueris
Carnis deliciis, ac assuescas quoque prauis,
Taliter artatur uia que paucis reperitur.

Dicit dominus in ewangelio: *Contendite intrare per angustam portam, quia arta est uia que ducit ad uitam et pau⟨c⟩a inueniunt eam. Et lata est uia et spaciosa que ducit ad mortem, et multi intrant per eam.* His datur intelligi quod uia mala patet omnibus et ultro offertur. Sed uia que ducit ad uitam non ita patet omnibus, nec sic ultro offertur, sed sollicite querenda est ut inueniatur. Sed licet hec uia sit arta, ingresso fit lata consuetudine boni, bona spe, caritate. Sed hanc faciunt artam terrene felicitatis iocunditas, carnis humane fragilitas, consuetudo mali. **[2–6]**

uia: Scilicet uia que uehit ad uitam. **[6]**

46. De timore

Non naturalem poteris remouere timorem,
Sed tu seruilem procul a te pelle timorem. *105v*

44 2 *triplex[1]*: there is, exceptionally, no caesura in this line; the text may be defective.

45 7–10 *Contendite… eam*: a paraphrase of Mt 7:13–14 and Lc 13:24

45.4 frueris: *another hand adds* uel ⟨fru⟩a⟨ris⟩ *above the line*

Absit mundanus timor humanusque. Timendus
Est deus ut castum metuit bona sponsa maritum.
Hic perfectorum timor est. Timor est aliorum
Vtilis, in talem ductor plerumque timorem.

[2] Hoc uerbum 'timeo' ex diuersis adiunctis diuersis modis accipitur. Dicitur 'timeo penam,' id est 'horreo penam'; 'timeo culpam,' id est 'caueo culpam'; 'timeo deum,' id est 'reuereor deum.' Hec acceptiones possunt haberi in memoria per hunc uersum:

Fit 'timet' adiunctis 'horret,' 'cauet,' et 'reueretur.'

Est itaque quidam timor horror, sed est horror moderatus et est horror immoderatus. Moderatus, scilicet naturalis horror proueniens ex natura, que corrupta est, quia ante corruptionem nature et ante peccatum Ade non erat huiusmodi timor. Sed postquam peccauit Adam, timuit et abscondit se. Huiusmodi timor, scilicet naturalis, est indifferens: nec est meritorius, nec demeritorius. Et huiusmodi timor erat etiam in Cristo, de sensualitate tantum et non de ratione. Nullus homo caret huiusmodi timore.

[3] Secundum quod 'timet' dicitur 'reueretur,' triplex est timor: seruilis siue ancillaris, inicialis, castus timor siue filialis. Seruilis timor est quando aliquis timet tantum propter penam uitandam et non propter amorem aliquem. Huiusmodi timorem habere solet seruus et ancilla, qui propter uerbera uitanda timent dominos et non propter amorem. Et ideo huiusmodi timor dicitur seruilis siue ancillaris. Iste timor cohibet manum, non animum; non potest esse sine mortali peccato, quia non potest esse cum caritate. Ille qui seruiliter timet non est absque mortali peccato; non tamen mortaliter peccat ex hoc quod seruiliter timet, quia seruiliter timere bonum est, scilicet utile, et effectus seruilis timoris bonus est, id est utilis, quia carere pena utile est. Sed finis seruilis timoris malus est, quia

46 13 *Fit…reueretur*: a similar verse can be found in William de Montibus, *Versarius*, under 'Timor' (fol. 113v).

18 *timuit…se*: cf. Gen 3:10; above, 33.53–54.

46.6 perfectorum *subst. for* persectorum *MS* **46.11** memoria: et *add. MS before corr.* **46.14** est horror *corr. in MS from* horror est **46.35** utile *corr. in MS from* utilis

respicere ad Gehennam, et tantum propter illam penam uitandam timere, malum est. Et cuius finis malus, ipsum malum est. Et ita seruilis timor est quoddam malum, scilicet non est meritorium uite. Dicitur quandoque quod seruilis timor introducit caritatem; dicitur quandoque expellere caritatem. Quod si intelligitur, introducit occasionaliter, expellit causaliter.

Horror siue timor immoderatus est mundanus uel humanus. [4]
Mundanus est quando aliquis supra modum timet dispendium rerum temporalium. Humanus est quando aliquis supra modum timet afflictionem corporis. Quem timorem habentes, etiam quidam sancti, lapsi sunt. Huiusmodi timor prohibitus est ubi dicitur: *Nolite timere eos qui occidunt corpus*, etc. Horror itaque siue timor inmoderatus, mundanus siue humanus, detestabilis est; non potest esse sine mortali peccato.

Castus timor siue filialis est quando aliquis timet deum pro [5]
amore iusticie, exclusa formidine pene, scilicet timet separari a deo sicut casta sponsa timet separari a casto sponso; et ideo dicitur 'castus.' Vel timet offendere deum, quo more bonus filius timet offendere patrem; et ideo dicitur 'filialis.' De habentibus filialem timorem dicitur:

> Oderunt peccare boni uirtutis amore.

De habentibus seruilem timorem dicitur:

> Oderunt peccare mali formidine pene.

hic perfectorum timor: Scilicet huiusmodi timor—cuiusmodi [6]

36 *respicere ad Gehennam*: cf. Gregory the Great, *Moralia in Iob* 31.37.76 (CCSL 143b:1603, lines 11–16).

37–38 *Et…est*[1]: cf. Boethius's translation of Aristotle, *Topica* 2.9, 114b20 (ed. Minio-Paluello, 5.1:46, line 1) *supra modum*: 'beyond the ordinary' (*DMLBS* s.v. *supra* 10b).

47 *Nolite…corpus*: Mt 10:28

56 *Oderunt…amore*: Horace, *Epistulae* 1.16.52

58 *Oderunt…pene*: a medieval addition to the above verse; see the critical apparatus in the editions of Klinger or Borzsák.

46.38 scilicet *corr. in MS from* sed **46.41** occasionaliter expellit: *the scribe began to write* -aliter e- *in MS in a different location before erasing it and completing the line elsewhere to provide more room for the verse below* **46.48–49** detestabilis *corr. in MS from* destabie **46.54** timet *written twice in ms before corr.*

timore timet casta sponsa castum maritum—est tantum perfectorum.

timor est aliorum: Scilicet inicialis timor est quorumdam aliorum qui sunt in caritate inperfecta.

Initialis timor est quando aliquis partim pro pena uitanda, partim pro amore iusticie timet, magis tamen pro amore iusticie. [7] Hic timor est in caritate licet inperfecta, et habet initium filialis timoris; et ideo dicitur 'initialis timor.' Dicit Iohannes: *Caritas foras mittit timorem*, scilicet caritas quantulacumque eliminat timorem mundanum et humanum et seruilem; uel 'caritas foras mit⟨tit⟩ ti⟨morem⟩,' scilicet caritas perfecta eli⟨minat⟩ etiam inicialem timorem.

47. Hic notatur quandoque exceptionem faciat hic dictio 'nisi' in quibusdam constructionibus

Per 'nisi' tollantur que his duo SPAR SE notatur.

Dictio 'nisi' quandoque tollit separata a proposito. Dicit Paulus: [3] *Nemini quicquam debeatis, nisi ut inuicem diligatis*. Non hic tolluntur ea que possunt haberi cum caritate, sed ea que separata sunt a caritate et non possunt haberi cum caritate. Quandoque tollit anthonomasiam: *Nemo bonus nisi deus unus*. Hic per hanc dictionem 'nisi' excluditur bonitas a qualibet re alia a deo, sed tollitur excellentia bonitatis a qualibet re alia a deo. Quandoque hec dictio 'nisi' excludit euidentiam. Nunc Cristus: *Generatio praua et peruersa signum querit, et non dabitur ei nisi signum Ione prophete*. Alia signa quam signum Ione

68–69 *Caritas…timorem*: 1 Io 4:18

47 1 cf. William de Montibus, *Tropi*, under 'Nisi' (Goering, *William de Montibus*, 364).
5 *Nemini…diligatis*: Rom 13:8
8 *anthonomasiam* = *antonomasiam*
Nemo…unus: Mc 10:18
11 *Nunc*: contrasting Moses' use of the same phrase above, 39.86–87
12–13 *Generatio…prophete*: Mt 12:39 or 16:4, conflated with Deut 32:5

47.4 dictio: *a lacuna of three to four letters precedes this word in MS* | a proposito *subst. for* apposito *MS*

prophete data erant de Cristo, sed nullum euidentius signum datum erat de morte eius et resurrectione, et in eo quod erat signum resurrectionis Cristi erat signum deitatis eius, quia in gloriosa resur⟨rectione⟩ apparuit eius deitas. Etiam per hanc dictionem 'nisi' tollitur hic euidentia. Signum datum erat de Cristo quando commutauit aquam in uinum, et ad hoc quando locutus est eis daturus erat signum in hoc quod ascenderet ad celos. Quandoque per hanc dictionem 'nisi' tolluntur

S Separata S Signa,
P Proposito, E Euidentia.
A Anthonomasia
R Rebus,

48. Ex his potest intelligi quibus de causis flagellet deus homines

Torquentur uariis homines plerique flagellis: *106r*
Augeat ut meritum pacientia, uel malefactum
Sic castigetur, aut uirtus sic teneatur
Et bene seruetur, aut ut per talia detur
Nosse salutiferi miracula maxima Cristi,
Aut ut perpetue fiat perceptio pene.

Quinque de causis flagellantur homines. Quandoque aliquis **[3–8]** flagellatur ut sic in eo augeatur meritum: ita deus ex habundanti gratia flagellauit Iob ut in eo augeretur meritum per pacientiam. Quandoque flagellatur aliquis ut in eo castigetur peccatum; sic flagellata est Maria soror Moysi, que cum Aaron obiurgauit ei propter Ethiopissam quam duxerat (siue ductam dimiserat); uel obiurgauit ei propter Sephoram uxorem eius, que rixata est

19 *commutauit...uinum*: cf. Io 2:1–10.
20–21 *locutus...celos*: cf. Io 6:62.

48 10 *habundanti = abundanti*
13–18 *Maria...sanitas*: Num. 12; cf. Gratian, C.2 q.7 d.p. c.27.

47.20 ascenderet *corr. in MS from* ascenderat **48.1** his *om. MS before corr.; add. above the line* **48.3** plerique: qe *add. ms before corr.* **48.9** quandoque *subst. for* quia *MS* **48.13** moysi *corr. in marg. from* aaron *MS*

cum ea. Et propter illam obiurgationem percussa est lepra, et fuit leprosa ·vii· diebus, et postea precibus Moysi restaurata est ei sanitas. Quandoque flagellatur aliquis ut in eo sic seruentur uirtutes: ita flagellatus est Paulus, cui datus est stimulus carnis sue, angelus Sathane qui eum colaphizauit, ne magnitudo reuelationum eum extolleret, sed in eo conseruaretur humilitas. Quandoque flagellatur aliquis ad hoc ut manifestetur gloria dei per ipsum: ita quidam natus cecus flagellatus est in hoc quod caruit uisu a natiuitate sua. Et hoc in eo actum est ut manifestaretur gloria dei in ipso. Vnde in ewangelio dicit Cristus de illo: *Neque hic peccauit nec parentes eius, sed ut manifestentur opera dei in ipso*. Quandoque flagellatur aliquis ut in presenti uita incipiat pena sua et perduret in eternum: ita flagellatus est Herodes et plures alii reprobi. Ex his intelligi potest quod omnis diuina percussio aut in nobis presentis uite est correctio aut inicium pene sequentis. Dicitur etiam quod deus aliquid punierit propter misterium. Dicitur etiam quandoque punire ad designationem humane infirmitatis: ita puniuntur infantes baptizati, ut per hoc detur intelligi quod magna est humana infirmitas.

49. In his ostenditur ad que ualeant opera misericordie facta ab eo qui peccato mortali constringitur

Culpa mortali dum sis omittere noli
Que pia sunt opera. Minuetur in his tibi pena,
Aut his tu poteris cicius desistere prauis,
Aut erit hac uita tibi merces inde soluta.

Opera misericordie que facit homo dum est in mortali peccato [3–6] non sunt meritoria uite eterne, sed ualent ad celeriorem conuersionem, quia si dat elemosinam pauperibus et dat libenter ea que instituti sunt, sicut decimas et oblationes, precibus pau-

19–20 *datus... colaphizauit*: cf. 2 Cor 12:7.
26–27 *Neque... ipso*: Io 9:3
28–29 *flagellatus est Herodes*: cf. Act 12:23; above, 40.53.

49 10 *decimas et oblationes*: cf. above, 2.40.

49.2 peccato *subst. for* peccata *MS*

perum et illorum qui sunt in ecclesia celerius poterit conuerti ad dominum. Valent et ad temporalium remunerationem, quia deus quandoque his qui sunt in mortali peccato dat mercedem in temporalibus bonis pro operibus misericordie que fecerunt. In ewangelio dictum est diuiti: *Memento quod recepisti bona in uita tua.* Ex hoc intelligi potest quod aliquid boni fecit, pro quo bona temporalia in mercedem recepit in uita sua et ad pene mitigationem, quia non tantum punietur quantum ille qui, in mortali peccato iacens, opera pietatis fatere renuit.

in his: Id est per hoc. **[4]**

50. De cruce domini ferenda

In cruce tollenda que sunt tibi semper habenda *106v*
Hec ('r' sublato) per VESCARVM memorato.

In cruce est seria ueritas, et non uanitas et uoluptas; et in cruce **[2]** est excensio menbrorum, et firma et fixa stabilitas, et coaptatio, et altitudo, et uniuersitas menbrorum. Itaque qui uult ferre crucem domini in se debet habere seriam ueritatem, et non uanitatem et uoluptatem. Debet etiam habere menbra excensa ad bonorum operum excercicia. Debet etiam habere firmam et fixam stabilitatem ne dimittat locum suum in quo proficit. Debet etiam habere coaptationem, scilicet ita coaptare se cruci ut possit sustinere. Debet uersare

15–16 *Memento…tua*: Lc 16:25; *memento quod* for *recordare quia* is found in Bernard of Clairvaux, *Sermo de conuersione ad clericos*, textus longior 21 (ed. Leclercq and Rochais, 4:94, line 2).

50 3 *r*: for scansion, understand *ēr*; cf. above, 30.3.
5 *excensio = extensio*
9 *excercicia = exercicia*
12–14 *uersare…humeri*: Horace, *Ars poetica* 39–40; the same adaptation of 'uersare' for Horace's 'uersate' is found in Peter the Chanter, *Verbum adbreuiatum*, textus conflatus 1.52 (CCCM 196:349, lines 198–199); textus prior 47 (CCCM 196a:311, lines 96–97); textus

50.4 est *subst. for* etiam *MS*

diu quid ferre recusent,
Quid ualeant humeri.

Non debet supra uires suas tot et tantis operibus insistere ut pre nimia multitudine operum et nimia difficultate tedio affectus labori succumbant; et ita debilitetur qui de cetero minus fortis sit siue debilis ad labores tolerandos. Debet etiam habere altitudinem, scilicet non descendere ad friuola mundi et uana et transitoria, attendens quod Cristus de cruce noluit descendere quando Iudei dicebant: *Si filius dei est, descendat de cruce*, etc. Sanctus quoque Andreas, nolens de cruce descendere, petiit ut non dimitteretur de cruce, nisi prius exspirasset. Debet etiam qui fert crucem domini in cruce habere uniuersitatem menbrorum, quia non sufficit ad optinendum uitam eternam quedam menbra ab illicitis operibus retrahere, ubi uniuersa menbra seruentur. Non bene custoditur ciuitas nisi undique muniatur, ita quod in nullo loco pateat hostibus aditus. Tripliter dicitur ferri crux domini: effusione sanguinis in martyrio, mortificatione carnis, compassione erga proximos.

In cruce Cristi baiulanda debet esse [3]
V Veritas,
E Exscensio,
S Stabilitas,
C Coaptatio,

---

alter 44 (CCCM 196b:221, lines 157–158).

21 *Si…cruce*: Mt 27:40; the phrasing in the third person is found in many writings of Augustine.

22–23 *Sanctus…exspirasset*: cf. Peter the Chanter, *Summa de sacramentis et animae consiliis* 3.50.340 (ed. Dugauquier, 3.2a:418, lines 34–41).

24–25 *uniuersitatem menbrorum*: this phrase is used infrequently (in comparison, for instance, to *uniuersitas gentium*); see for instance John of Salisbury, *Policraticus* 6.25 (ed. Webb, 2:73, line 29) and Gerald of Wales, *Speculum ecclesiae* 4.13 (ed. Brewer, 287). (On William de Montibus's use of the *Policraticus*, see Dines, 'The Earliest Use of John of Salisbury's *Policraticus*,' 109–111.)

27–28 *Non…aditus*: cf. above, 40.64–66.

28 *Tripliter* = *tripliciter* (cf. *multipliter* above, 17.3.)

50.17 qui *subst. for* quod *MS* **50.23** exspirasset *corr. in MS from* expirasset

A Altitudo,
R
V Vniuersitas
M Menbrorum.

51. De septem uiciis capitalibus siue principalibus, ex quibus alia uicia oriuntur

Crimine manantes sunt tres et bis duo fontes:
Tu per AGI LAICI qui sunt poteris reminisci.

·Vii· sunt uicia capitalia siue principalia, ut ait Gregorius super [3]
Exodum: auari⟨ci⟩a, inanis gloria, luxuria, accidia siue tristicia, ira, castrimargia, inuidia. Hec uicia significata sunt, ut ait Crisostomus, in ·vii· populis qui terram promissionis Israeli promissam tenebant: de his, quasi ·vii· fontibus, cuncte animarum mortifere corruptele emanant. Et dicuntur hec 'capitalia,' quia ex eis oriuntur omnia mala. Nullum enim malum est quod non ab aliquo horum originem trahat.

Per litteras istarum dictionum—'agi,' 'laici'—possunt haberi [4]
in memoria ·vii· uicia capitalia, que sunt hec:

A Auaricia, L Luxuria,
G Gloria A Accidia,
I Inanis, I Ira,
C Castrimargia,
I Inuidia.

52. In his datur intelligi que contemplatiue uite et que actiue uite conueniant

Vt grates donet, legat et meditetur et oret,
Contemplatiuum decet, et calcare tumultum.
Congruit actiuis aliis dare uerba saluti;

51 5–12 *·Vii·…trahat*: adapted from Peter Lombard, *Sententiae* 2.42.6
7 *castrimargia* = *gastrimargia*, 'gluttony'

51.1 principalibus *corr. in MS from* principialibus **52.1** datur *corr. in MS from* datis

Ecclesie sacris celebratio congruit illis.
Est opus actiui pariter peregre proficisci,
Bisque duas et tres horas seruare reales.

Quatuor sunt partes uite contemplatiue: gratitudo, lectio, meditatio, oratio. Dicitur quod in futuro cessabunt lectio, meditatio, oratio, sed gratitudo erit in futuro, quia sancti in futuro referent gratias deo de saluatione sua. [3–4]

tumultum: Tumultum carnis, mundi, diaboli, et prauorum hominum. [4]

Quatuor sunt partes actiue uite: predicatio, peregrinatio, sacramentorum celebratio, operum misericordie exibitio. [5–6]

·Vii· reales hore dicuntur ·vii· opera misericordie, quorum ·vi· designat dominus in ewangelio ubi dicit: *Esuriui, et dederunt mihi manducare*, etc. Septimum commendatur in Thobia de sepultura mortuorum. ·Vii· uocales hore dicuntur matutine et prima et tercia, etc. He hore cantantur in ecclesia; ideo dicuntur uocales hore. [8]

52 7 *peregre proficisci*: glossed *peregrinatio* in the commentary

17 *reales hore*: the distinction between *reales* and *uocales hore* is found in works associated with the theological schools of Paris in the second half of the twelfth century. It is used by William de Montibus, *Numerale* 7.1 (Goering, *William de Montibus*, 255); *Versarius*, under 'Hore' (fol. 57v). The concept as expressed here is similar to Peter the Chanter, *Verbum adbreuiatum*, textus conflatus, 1.77 (CCCM 196:525, lines 330–336); cf. textus alter, 55 and 63 (CCCM 196b:277, lines 163–169; 323, lines 231–243); the same ideas are presented without the idea of the hours in his *Summa de sacramentis et animae consiliis* 2.2.3.126–127 (ed. Dugauquier, 2:255–261). See also Peter of Poiters, *Summa de confessione* 55-a, 55-b (CCCM 51:78, lines 73–77; 82–83, lines 187–191); Gerald of Wales, *Vita S. Hugonis* 1.6 (ed. Dimock, 98); and Thomas of Chobham, *Summa de arte praedicandi* 2 (CCCM 82:29, lines 359–266).

18–19 *Esuriui…manducare*: Mt 25:35 (*dederunt* for Vulg. *dedistis*)

20–21 *sepultura mortuorum*: cf. Tob 1:20–2:9, 4:3, 12:12.

52.7 peregre *subst. (as suggested by Dinkova-Bruun) for* peregere *MS*
52.15 peregrinatio *corr. in MS from* peregrignatio

53. De superbia cauenda

Neue tibi tribuas bona si qua tenes, neque credas 107r
Pro meritis tribui si desuper hec tibi tradi
Credas. Nec bona que desunt iactabis habere,
Nec spretis aliis specialiter ut uidearis
Indulgere bonis cupias: sic namque superbis.

Inicium omnis peccati est superbia, que est amor proprie excellentie; cuius ·iiii·^{or} sunt species, ut ait Gregorius: Prima est, cum bonum quod habet quis sibi tribuit; secunda, cum credit a deo esse datum, sed tamen pro suis meritis; tercia, cum iactat se bonum habere quod non habet; quarta, cum ceteris despectis singulariter uult uideri appetere bona que ipse habet. Scilicet si tribuas bona tibi, non deo, uel si credas bona tribui pro meritis et non gratis, uel si iactes te habere bona que non habes, uel si appetis uideri specialiter appetere bona spretis aliis, superbia est. [2–6]

54. Hic notatur quod necessaria est coniunctio spei et timoris

Ex spe prorumpit presumptio, si timor absit;
Desperare facit sine spe tibi, si timor assit.
Vt tibi coniuncti prosint, spem iunge timori,
Neue per aspera spem tollas, per blanda timorem.

In psalmo dicitur: *Ecce oculi domini super metuentes eum, et in eis qui sperant super misericordia eius.* Et alibi dicitur: *Beneplacitum est domino super timentes eum, et in eis qui sperant super misericordia eius.* Ex his potest intelligi quod necessaria est coniunctio spei et timoris, quia spes sine timore facit hominem presumptuosum et temerarium. Timor sine spe facit hominem pusillanimem et desperantem. Spes et timor sunt due mole, inter quas moli debet omnis Cristianus, ut fiat panis [2–4]

53 7–12 *Inicium…uideri*: Peter Lombard, *Sententiae* 2.42.7.1–2

54 6–7 *Ecce…eius*: Ps 32:18
7–9 *Beneplacitum…eius*: Ps 146:11
12–14 *Spes…sibi*: cf. Gregory the Great, *Moralia in Iob* 33.12.24 (CCSL 143b:1694, lines 80–82) and Peter the Chanter, *Verbum adbreuiatum*, textus conflatus 2.24 (CCCM 196:688, lines 139–140); textus alter 80 (CCCM 196b:420, lines 103–104).

esibilis deo quem deus trahiciat in se ut uniatur sibi. De his molis dicit Moyses: *Non accipies loco pignoris superiorem molam siue inferiorem*, id est, Non auferes alicui spem uel timorem.

Non debet aliquis concipere in animo tantum esse rigorem iusticie dei ut sibi auferat spem, nec debet ita blandiri sibi de misericordia dei ut auferat sibi timorem. Et si aliquis conueniat alium in confessione de peccatis suis, ille cui alius confitetur peccata non debet ita rigide loqui de iusticia dei ut auferat ei spem, nec debet ita blandienter loqui de misericordia dei aut auferat ei timorem. [5]
tollas: Tibi uel alii.

55. De uoto

Quoddam discrete quoddam uotum fit inepte. *107v*
Votum discretum commune uel est speciale;
Est et priuatum sollempneue consiliiue.
Quomodo discreto fiet promissio uoto
Redditioque, notent CIRCVMVEHO DEMO CAVEFAC.

Votum [2]
inepte: *Temerarium*
Ecclesiastes: *Ne te temere quid loquaris*. Glosa est: Vouendo deo.
Arguitur inepte, quia uotum fecit inepte. Fuit enim secundum Iosephum in uouendo stultus, et in soluendo impius.

14 *esibilis*: 'edible'
trahiciat = *traiciat*
15–16 *Non...inferiorem*: Deut 24:6

55 1 This section is of a different character from the rest of the work. The commentary is set out in a format akin to a modern outline, and exceptionally includes specific biblical references. On the rhyming schemes of the verse, see the introduction. For a fuller description of categories used here, see Peter the Chanter, *Summa de sacramentis et animae consiliis* 3.6.224 (ed. Dugauquier, 3a:200–206).
9–10 *Ne...deo*: Eccl 5:1 and its *Glosa interl.*
11–12 *Fuit...impius*: Peter Comestor, *Historia scholastica: Libri Iudicium* 12 (PL 198:1284c)

55.11 inepte[1] *corr. in MS from* iepte

Ysidorus: In malis promissis rescinde fidem; in turpi uoto muta decretum. Quod incaute uouisti, ne facias; inpia est promissio que scelere adimpletur.

Discretum **[3]**

Commune, generale, prime, et absolute necessitatis, ut uotum baptismale: sine hoc non est salus.

Speciale emergentis necessitatis, ut promiss⟨i⟩o penitentialis. In hoc etiam qualitas actionis exigitur: *Facite dignos fructus penitentie*, scilicet in caritate; alioquin penitentia est iteranda uel commutanda ad arbitrium sacerdotis.

Singulare **[4]**

Consilii et perfectionis, ut uotum uirginitatis, monachationis, et huiusmodi. In hoc sufficit substantia actionis.

Priuatum
- Loco priuato
- Coram deo, tantum } in abscondito factum
- Coram paucis
- Sollempnitatibus destitutum

Sollempne
- In facie ecclesie
- Quod faciunt
  - Presentia sacerdotis
  - Scriptura professionis
  - Ordinis susceptio
  - Habitus assumptio

Votum discretum **[5]**

In promissione

Ex circumspectione

Cum deliberatione. Ecclesiastes ·x·: *Non sit cor tuum uelox ad proferendum coram deo sermonem*. Glosa: Voti.

13–15 *Ysidorus…adimpletur*: Peter Lombard, *Sententiae* 3.39.9.2; Gratian, C.22 q.4 c.5

20–21 *Facite…penitentie*: Lc 3:8

24 *monachationis*: 'of becoming a monk'

41 *Ecclesiastes ·x·*: the biblical citations used here appear to use a system local to Lincoln.

41–42 *Non…Voti*: Eccl 5:1 and its *Glosa interl.*

Cum moderatione. Ecclesiastes ·x·: *Ne dederis os tuum ut peccare facias carnem tuam.* Glosa: Ne ultra quam potes uoueas.

In honestate

Votum enim est testificatio quedam promissionis spontanee, que deo et de his que dei sunt proprie fieri debet. Vel sic: Votum est pollicitatio meritis facta deo de his que ad religionem pertinent. Vel sic: Votum est conceptio melioris boni, animi deliberatione firmata.

In ueritate

Ne quis ficte uoueat, sed implere proponat. Ecclesiastes ·x·: *Displicet deo infidelis et stulta promissio*, id est promissio non impleta et proinde indiscreta.

Cum conditione

Nisi impediat

Necessitas

Illicitudo

Quantum in uouente est

Per gratiam dei

Sub auctoritate

Ecclesie precipientis. Numeri ·lxv· pater reuocat uotum filie familias, et uix uxoris quam cito audierat. Et Or⟨igenes⟩ ait: Si qua anima uouet aliquid propere et minus apte, custodis est reprimere uouentis audaciam et retundere.

43–45 *Ne…uoueas*: Eccl 5:5 and its *Glosa interl.*

47–48 *Votum…debet*: Peter Lombard, *Sententiae* 4.38.1

49–50 *Votum…pertinent*: cf. Peter Lombard, *Sententiae* 4.38.2.5.

50–51 *Votum…firmata*: this definition occurs in the gloss to contemporary manuscripts of Gratian, C.27 q.1: see Schulte, *Decretistarum jurisprudentiae specimen*, 16; Kuttner and Rathbone, 'Anglo-Norman Canonists of the Twelfth Century,' 349–350; Brundage, *Medieval Canon Law and the Crusader*, 54 n. 99 and 57 n. 115.

54 *Displicet…promissio*: Eccl 5:3

59 *Illicitudo*: 'unlawfulness' (cf. *iniquitas* above, 7.14.)

63–64 *pater…audierat*: cf. Num 30:4–13.

65–66 *Si…retundere*: *Glosa marg.* to Num 30:3, quoting Origen (from the translation of Rufinus), *In Numeros homiliae* 24.3 (ed. Baehrens, 2:231, lines 28–30)

55.46 in honestate *subst. for* inhoneste *MS* **55.64** origenes *corr. in MS from* oratio

Dei reuelantis. Augustinus ait: Beata Maria uouit se perseueratura uirginem, nisi deus ei aliter reuelaret.

In uocis emissione

Deuter⟨onomium⟩ ·cxv·: *Quod semel egressum est de labiis, obseruabis, et facies quod promisisti domino tuo et propria uoluntate et ore tuo locutus es.* Et in psalmo: *Reddam tibi uota mea que distinxerunt labia mea.*

In reditione [6]

Accelerat⟨i⟩one

Deuter⟨onomium⟩ ·cxv·: *Cum uotum uoueris deo, non tardabis reddere.* Ecclesiaste⟨s⟩ ·xi·: *Si quid uouisti deo, ne moreris reddere*, tamen cito fit quod commode fit.

Fidelitate

Res uotiua reddatur in

Se. Mattheus: *Relinque ibi munus tuum ante altare.* G⟨losa⟩: Non ait, Refer quod recte offertur; immutari non licet, id est pretermitti.

Equipollenti. Le⟨uiticus⟩ ·lxix·viii· uota sub estimatione redimuntur. Et Ge⟨nesis⟩ ·lxx·vii· Ioseph pro pecunia accepit commutationem pecorum. Et detur D. ·lxxxii·: Ieiunium psalterio uel denario operarii redimitur.

Maiori. Minora redimuntur per altiora et artiora. Inferius enim continetur in superiori, et minus soluitur in maiori.

Caritate

Omnia uestra in caritate fiant, presertim promissio penitentialis, ut penitens faciat dignos fructus penitentie.

67–68 *Beata…reuelaret*: Gratian, C.27 q.2 d.p. c.2
70–72 *Quod…es*: Deut 23:23
73 *Reddam…mea*[2]: Ps 65:13–14
76–77 *Cum…reddere*: Deut 23:21
77–78 *Si…reddere*: Eccl 5:3
81 *Relinque…altare*: Mt 5:24
84–85 *uota…redimuntur*: cf. Lev 27:15–19.
85–86 *Ioseph…pecorum*: Gen 47:15–17
87–88 *Ieiunium…redimitur*: Gratian, D.82 c.5
93 *Omnia…fiant*: 1 Cor 16:14
94 *dignos…penitentie*: cf. above, lines 20–21.

Votum discretum:

CIRCVM	Circum-spectione	VE	Veritate,	DE	Deliberatione,
		HO	Honest⟨at⟩e	MO	Moderat⟨i⟩one,

C Conditione,
A Auctoritate,
V Vocis
E Emissione,
F Fidelitate,
A Accelerat⟨i⟩o⟨n⟩e,
C Caritate.

55.100 uocis *corr. in MS from* uoccis

INDEX OF SCRIPTURAL REFERENCES

References are keyed to sections and line numbers of *Ex diuersis auditis*.

TORONTO MEDIEVAL LATIN TEXTS

1 *Three Lives of English Saints*, ed. Michael Winterbottom (1972)
2 *The Gospel of Nicodemus*, ed. H.C. Kim (1973)
3 *Peter the Venerable: Selected Letters*, ed. Janet Martin (1974)
4 *A Thirteenth-Century Anthology of Rhetorical Poems*, ed. Bruce Harbert (1975)
5 *Two Alcuin Letter-Books*, ed. Colin Chase (1975)
6 *Three Latin Comedies*, ed. Keith Bate (1976)
7 *The Life of Gundulf, Bishop of Rochester*, ed. Rodney Thomson (1977)
8 *Boccaccio: In Defence of Poetry. Genealogiae deorum gentilium liber XIV*, ed. Jeremiah Reedy (1978)
9 *Bartholomaeus Anglicus: On the Properties of Soul and Body. De proprietatibus rerum libri III et IV*, ed. R. James Long (1979)
10 *Selected Sermons of Stephen Langton*, ed. Phyllis B. Roberts (1980)
11 *Philippe de Mézières' Campaign for the Feast of Mary's Presentation*, ed. William E. Coleman (1981)
12 *The Canterbury Hymnal*, ed. Gernot R. Wieland (1982)
13 *The Rule of St Benedict: The Abingdon Copy*, ed. John Chamberlin (1982)
14 *Robert Grosseteste: Templum Dei*, ed. Joseph Goering and F.A.C. Mantello (1984)
15 *The Oxford Poems of Hugh Primas and the Arundel Lyrics*, ed. C.J. McDonough (1984)
16 *Avitus: The Fall of Man. De spiritalis historiae gestis libri I–III*, ed. Daniel J. Nodes (1985)
17 *Nigel of Canterbury: Miracles of the Virgin Mary, in verse. Miracula sancte Dei genitricis virginis Marie, versifice*, ed. Jan Ziolkowski (1986)
18 *A Durham Book of Devotions*, ed. Thomas H. Bestul (1987)
19 *Speeches from the Oculus pastoralis*, ed. Terence O. Tunberg (1990)
20 *The 'Vulgate' Commentary on Ovid's Metamorphoses: The Creation Myth and the Story of Orpheus*, ed. Frank T.

Coulson (1991)

21 *Richard Rolle: Emendatio vitae; Orationes ad honorem nominis Ihesu*, ed. Nicholas Watson (1995)

22 *Latin Colloquies from Pre-Conquest Britain*, ed. Scott Gwara (1996)

23 *Stella clericorum*, ed. Eric H. Reiter (1997)

24 *Fra Nicola da Milano: Collationes de beata virgine*, ed. M. Michèle Mulchahey (1997)

25 *The Fables of 'Walter of England*,' ed. Aaron E. Wright (1997)

26 *A Book of British Kings: 1200 BC–1399 AD*, ed. A.G. Rigg (2000)

27 *Saints' Lives by Walter of Châtillon: Brendan, Alexis, Thomas Becket*, ed. Carsten Wollin (2002)

28 *The Ancestry of Jesus: Excerpts from Liber generationis Iesu Christi filii Dauid filii Abraham (Matthew 1:1–17)*, ed. Greti Dinkova-Bruun (2005)

29 *The Deposition of Richard II: 'The Record and Process of the Renunciation and Deposition of Richard II' (1399) and Related Writings*, ed. David R. Carlson (2007)

30 *An Epitome of Biblical History: Glosses on Walter of Châtillon's Alexandreis 4.176–274*, ed. David Townsend (2008)

31 *The Sermons of William of Newburgh*, ed. A.B. Kraebel (2010)

32 *Peter Abelard: Historia calamitatum. Consolation to a Friend*, ed. Alexander Andrée (2015)

33 *Samuel Presbiter: Notes from the School of William de Montibus*, ed. Andrew N.J. Dunning (2016)